Transforming History

Also by William Irwin Thompson

The Imagination of an Insurrection
At the Edge of History
Passages about Earth
Evil and World Order
Darkness and Scattered Light
The Time Falling Bodies Take to Light
Blue Jade from the Morning Star (poetry)
Islands out of Time (fiction)
Pacific Shift
Gaia: A Way of Knowing (editor)
Imaginary Landscape
Gaia Two: Emergence: The New Science of Becoming (editor)
Reimagination of the World (with David Spangler)
The American Replacement of Nature
Worlds Interpenetrating and Apart (poetry)
Coming into Being

Transforming History

A Curriculum for Cultural Evolution

William Irwin Thompson

LINDISFARNE BOOKS

Published by Lindisfarne Books
P.O. Box 799
Great Barrington, MA 01230
www.lindisfarne.org

Copyright © 2001 by William Irwin Thompson

The conclusion to chapter four of this book originally appeared in an earlier version in *The Journal of Consciousness Studies,* vol. 7, no. 7, May 2000.

Book design by ediType

Library of Congress Cataloging-in-Publication Data
Thompson, William Irwin.
    Transforming history: a curriculum for cultural evolution /
William Irwin Thompson.
        p. cm.
    Includes bibliographical references.
    ISBN 1-58420-001-4
    1. History – Study and teaching (Elementary) – United States.
    2. History – Study and teaching (Secondary) – United States.
    3. Home schooling – United States – Curricula.   I. Title.

LB1582.U6 T46 2001
907.1'273 – dc21

                                        2001029985

Printed in the United States of America

10 9 8 7 6 5 4 3 2 1

Dedicated to
Courtney Ross and Anders Holst
and their new life's work with
The Ross School and Institute

Contents

– O n e –

The Four Cultural-Ecologies
of the West

All descriptions of the past are *in* the present; therefore, history tells our descendants as much about us as it does about the imaginary creatures we call our ancestors. Like an image before us in the rearview mirror of a car, the picture of where we have been keeps changing as we move forward in space and time. The narratives of the past from even so short a time ago as the beginning of the twentieth century now no longer describe us, and thus each generation must reinvent the past to make it correspond to its sense of the present.

In much the same way, twentieth-century futurism was little more than a not very imaginative managerial description of the implications of its present. Futurology, like archaeology, was an academic way of closing down the past and the future so that they were no longer open to the imaginative expansion of the present. The space of the twentieth century was under the political control of technocratic management; so it was important that the thought police patrol the exits. With futurist Herman Kahn guarding the year 2000 c.e. and prehistorian Aubrey Burl guarding the year 2000 b.c.e., we were closed in and protected from any narrative of future or past that was not propaganda for the technological society.[1]

All of which is to say that the past and the future do not exist; nevertheless we need these narrative fictions, for we gain knowledge by looking backward at patterns and forward in anticipation of the results of our actions. We can live without a substantially real past or future, for our materialistic society is

1

more concerned with the immediate demands of the present; it is only when we find that the present doesn't exist absolutely either (for the very act of perceiving it takes away its definition by pushing it into the past) that we become disoriented. When we look down for a ground to our being, we find ourselves walking on water that reflects the sky.

Physics, of all sciences, was the first to deliver us from the illusion of the substantial reality of matter, and it was Heisenberg who pointed out more than two generations ago that we do not live in nature, but in a description of nature.[2] Coeval with Heisenberg's analysis of matter was Heidegger's analysis of being, which revealed the groundlessness of basing existence on a metaphysics of substance, on a substantial reality. (Notice that "reality," our very word for truth, comes from the Latin *res* and means "thing," so for us reality means "thingishness.")

Politicians like to pretend that these philosophical matters are obscure and need concern only professors of philosophy, but we have merely to watch the rock music videos of the young to realize that the multiple, interpenetrating spaces of the paintings of Magritte (as, for example, in his *L'enfance d'Icare*) became part of pop culture and the common imagery of music videos, starting with The Cars' "You Might Think I'm Crazy." Computers and video synthesizers have democratized epistemology. In industrial culture there is a left and a right, and a top and a bottom; but in electronic culture, top becomes pop, and left and right become replaced with the fast forward of futurists hyping a new robotics technology and the rewind of Sun Belt conservatives, trying to preserve suburban family values.

Music video put all human emotions into quotation marks, for it was clear that the love song was not expressing love, but was about "love." In the same way, the video imagery of war and apocalypse, whether sweetly sung by Boy George or screamed by Kiss, was not communicating an attraction or a revulsion to war; it was expressing a displacement from history. All history simply became visually grainy black and white quotes from old movies, whether Lang's *Metropolis* or Riefenstahl's *Triumph of the Will*, and in this displacement of consciousness from literate history to the now of electronic video, the young were doomed to Blake's "dull eternal round." We may not yet have Nietzsche's Eternal Return, but in North America we do have a cable culture of perpetual reruns.

Top and pop in culture, like past and future in the present, are the limbs of the body politic, and one cannot understand contemporary society merely by reading *The New York Review of Books* or watching MTV. An elite may define a self-conscious approach to culture through a literature, but a cultural-ecology is not a literary definition of a social group; it is a tissue of simultaneities of organisms playing out a similar adaptive approach in different contexts, different demes, different biomes. Heidegger may work to destruct metaphysics, and Derrida may follow him in an effort to destruct literary discourse, but even in Paris, *les enfants du rock* defer and displace automatically and unthinkingly, for the effect of putting all emotions into quotation marks in music video is to deconstruct the message with the medium. The content of the video clips is clearly banal and atrocious, but the content is not what is really going on.

The literary critic and the philosopher analyze a culture from within that culture's definition of culture.[3] The anthropologist, suffering from geographical displacement, labors to define the dynamics of culture from outside, but still carries within himself or herself a theory of dynamics and mechanics that he or she has borrowed from early European physics. The cultural ecologist, however, is more like *les enfants du rock* and working from a geographical and a psychological displacement, for he or she is displaced from the content of his or her own culture and from the content of anthropology's instructions on how to behave as a proper scientific anthropologist. Like an astronaut in space looking down on the earth from on high, or a mystic in meditation looking down on the mind from on high, the cultural-ecologist is displaced from the conventional ground of perception. All this would be extremely esoteric if technology had not democratized the experience, for the effect of personal computers and music videos is to put literate "civilization" into quotation marks.

This shift in sensibility, this transformation of mentality, is

a shift from what I call Atlantic, European, industrial civilization to Pacific, planetary, electronic culture. It is not a shift
caused by technology, for that kind of narration of linear causation derives from the old industrial habits of thought; it is
a shift in consciousness in which top culture and pop culture
are synchronously involved in the adaptive play of and within a
new cultural-ecology. In many ways, the older philosophers and
artists of Europe have foreshadowed the new culture in which
they would not feel at home.

The groundlessness of being opens up to us in the old-
fashioned books of Heidegger and the old-fashioned canvases
of Magritte. Different children will spend the family inheritance
of Europe in different ways; Ric Ocasek of The Cars moved
from canvas to video synthesizer, but Keiji Nishitani, a personal
student of Heidegger, moved from metaphysics to zazen to favor the kind of displacement described by Dogen Zenji as "the
dropping off of body and mind":

> True equality is not simply a matter of an equality of human
> rights and the ownership of property. Such equality con-
> cerns man as the subject of desires and rights and comes
> down, in the final analysis, to the self-centered mode of
> being of man himself. It has yet to depart fundamentally
> from the principle of self-love. And therein the roots of
> discord and strife lie ever concealed. True equality, on the
> contrary, comes about in what we might call the reciprocal
> interchange of absolute inequality, such that the self and
> the other stand simultaneously in the position of absolute
> master and absolute servant with regard to one another. It
> is an equality in love.
>
> Only on the field of emptiness does all this become pos-
> sible. Unless the thoughts and deeds of man one and all
> be located on such a field, the sorts of problems that beset
> humanity have no chance of ever really being solved.[4]

In the Kyoto School of Nishitani, the East reconceptualized
the West to show how the ultimate development of materialism
led to nihilism. But it takes no mirror made in Japan to make us

see that about ourselves, for we need only turn the pages of a history of Western painting to see the full story. We begin with Giotto, in whose work nature is merely a stage for a religious event, as in the *Flight into Egypt;* we pass on to Brueghel's *Conversion of Saint Paul,* where the religious event is not as large as the horse's behind; and then we continue on to the landscapes of Ruysdael, where the religious event has dropped out of the picture altogether; from there on the thingishness of reality gets very thick, with the still lifes of Kauw and the columnar temples of Poussin; but with Claude Lorrain the twilight over the temples becomes more important than the stones, and we begin to pass from matter into the mysteries of perception; and once into that psychological shift, there is no stopping until Monet's cathedrals melt and solid matter disappears into the emptiness of the Rothko *Chapel.* With the history of Western paintings before our mind's eye, we can literally see what Nishitani was talking about.

The movement from Heidegger to Nishitani was a Pacific Shift in philosophy,[5] but these Pacific Shifts are not limited to philosophy. The movement from Warren McCulloch to Humberto Maturana and Francisco Varela was a Pacific Shift in neurophysiology; in one the doctrine of materialism is negated, and in the other the doctrine of representationism in the nervous system was negated,[6] but in both cases it was the worldview of Atlantic civilization that was being set aside.

It is no cultural accident that both the Kyoto School of philosophy and the Santiago School of neurophysiology of Maturana and Varela shared a common Pacific orientation, and, in the case of Varela, an invocation of the relevance of Buddhism to postmodernist science. The Pacific has become the new Mediterranean, with a new relationship between religion and science that is as different from Protestantism and industrial science as Pythagoras's synthesis was from Mesopotamian astrology. Nishitani was a personal student of Heidegger, and Varela has been influenced by Heidegger's writings; but neither the Japanese philosopher nor the Chilean biologist have been content to rest with Heidegger's late Christian ontology. Both pushed on from a vestigial theology into an explicit a-theology of Buddhism. The end of the West becomes the ultimate shore of the East.

The philosophical works of Heidegger, Nishitani, and Varela are read by an international intellectual elite, but the cultural wave that brings the East to the West carries many other forms of life, and the California teenager who sits transfixed before the graphics of his personal computer is also participating in the cultural shift from the Protestant ethic and the spirit of capitalism to Zen and Tantric Buddhism and the spirit of cybernetics. Small wonder that the Dalai Lama has become popular with movie stars and a global superstar in his own right.

One of the most pioneering thinkers in this Pacific Shift was Gregory Bateson. As an anthropologist doing research among schizophrenics who lived outside normal reality, Bateson made the phrase "double bind" a household word. As a participant in the postwar Macy Conferences in New York,[7] which brought the pioneers of cybernetics together, Bateson was part of the creation of a new science. Bateson is important not only because of his contributions, but also because his own journey in the ecology of Mind also embodied Western culture's odyssey from Europe to California. He began his career at St. John's College, Cambridge, did his early fieldwork in Melanesia, but ended his days as the philosopher of the furthest edges of the European mentality. In the last years of his life, Governor Jerry Brown appointed him to the Board of Regents of the University of California, but Bateson continued to live with the counterculture both at Lindisfarne in New York and Esalen Institute in Big Sur. He died at the Zen Center in San Francisco in 1980, but Bateson was neither a leader of encounter groups nor zazen sessions; he simply liked to haunt edges to observe the movement across thresholds flash into "the difference that became information."[8]

The pattern that connects Bateson to Varela, and both to Buddhism, was a personal pattern of friendship, as well as the larger cultural pattern of transformation. Both of these theoreticians of the biology of knowledge shared a fascination with the groundlessness of Buddhism and the intellectual openness of the Pacific world. Both saw the mental habit of the West as one in which

Being is posited as *a* being and called "God"; in which process is arrested in substance and called "material reality"; and in which Mind is made into an organism without an environment and called "the self." For both Bateson and Varela, all three of these cultural activities are part of the same process of reification that isolates God from nature, mind from matter, and organism from the environment; and each ends up giving us a system of abstractions that we mistake for reality, to the destruction of both culture and nature.

In Bateson's now-classic analysis "The Effects of Conscious Purpose on Human Adaptation," these three mistakes of thinking are seen to be part of the maladaptation of civilization to nature:

> If consciousness has feedback upon the remainder of mind, and if consciousness deals only with a skewed sample of the events of the total mind, then there must exist a *systematic* (i.e., non-random) difference between the conscious views of self and the world, and the true nature of self and the world. Such a difference must distort the processes of adaptation.[9]

In the decades since Bateson delivered that lecture in Austria in 1968, the distortion in the process of adaptation has progressed to the point of a disruption about to become a catastrophe. As this catastrophe has already begun to become visible in the death of the forests in Europe and in global warming, this visibility of process is already changing the way we see history in the rearview mirror. Now it seems inappropriate to mark time with monuments to ego, such as Nelson's Column in Trafalgar Square; now a description of civilization is more truly read in the sequence of infrared photographs from space that show the Mediterranean's progress toward becoming an industrial sewer.

As we look back on the past in our contemporary imagination, we can see it as a movement from the Near Eastern Riverine cultural-ecology at the edge of the NASA Landsat photograph of the Middle East, to the Mediterranean cultural-ecology in the center, and, to the left, the Atlantic cultural-ecology of the European era. When we look down from on high with the eye of an astronaut, we cannot see the celebrated effects of egos with names and monuments; we can only see an action analogous to the presence of bacteria in a compost heap or of a mold in a Petri dish: the changes of color for the seas and the forests tell us of the deadly presence of highly toxic human institutions. Where in this collective action is the individual human will? Is the human being simply a catalytic agent secreted by Gaia in order to transform the subterranean oceans of oil into a moving gas in the earth's atmosphere? Is human consciousness, as Marx would say, a "false consciousness"? Could it be, in a strange blending of Marx and Buddha, that human beings do not—perhaps cannot—know what they are *doing*? Was Lewis Thomas closer to the ecological truth of symbiotic humanity when he observed that humans were moving toward fusion all the time that they kept mumbling about the self?

The interest that Buddhism held for scientists like Bateson and Varela makes sense. It is not simply a question of the West's discovery of the *groundlessness* of its emphasis on material reality, but also of the enormous growth of suffering in the expansion of industrial society known as economic development. Buddha's is the aboriginal questioning of the relationship between mind and suffering; so it is small wonder that as science approached the frontiers of mind in cognitive science, neurophysiology, and artificial intelligence, and as industrial society mass-produced human suffering, thinkers at the edge of European culture, such as Bateson, Nishitani, and Varela, noticed the relevance of the past of Buddhism to the future of science and philosophy.

Given the enormity of human suffering we now face in our overpopulated planet, and given the still-youthful vigor of science, I think that this relationship between Buddhism and science will be an enduring Pythagorean marriage and not a passing Romantic affair. The relationship between religion and science is so complex and elaborate that only a civilization is complex enough to elaborate it. Just such a new planetary civilization is emerging around the edges of the Pacific, and we can look back now to the past and see a movement from Riverine to Mediterranean to Atlantic precisely because the West is now passing out of the Atlantic cultural-ecology of Europe into the new cultural-ecology of the Pacific.

The historical movement from one cultural-ecology to another can be centuries long, as in the movement from Mesopotamian to classical to medieval; or it can be the journey of a lifetime, as in Bateson's movement from England to California; or it can become a metanoia in which the world is re-experienced by the individual in an instant. To appreciate the movement out of the old cultural-ecology into the new one, consider the experience of the astronaut Russell Schweickart, the first man to float in space without a vehicle to frame his perceptions. Because of a malfunction with his camera, Schweickart had a moment to *be* and not to *do;* in that instant he dropped the linear perspective of the box of his camera to comprehend the earth with his whole body and soul. In his remarks at the Lindisfarne Conference in Southampton in 1974, Schweickart described the experience in the following way:

> You look down there and you can't imagine how many borders and boundaries you cross, again and again and again. And you don't even see them. There you are—hundreds of people in the Mideast killing each other over some imaginary line that you can't see—and from where you see it, the thing is a whole, and it's so beautiful. You wish you could take one in each hand, one from each side in the various conflicts, and say, "Look! Look at that! What's important?"[10]

The world of industrial "man" is a world of *objects* separated by lines: mansions at one end, dioxin dumps at the other. But in the Pacific-Aerospace cultural-ecology, the world is known to be a field of interpenetrating *presences,* and in the world of space one is constrained to be on more intimate terms with one's waste. This is a knowledge that is brought back to earth, for aerospace technologies lead directly to new understandings of ecology. With satellites, one sees the life of rivers and seas; with space capsules and shuttles, one learns the placing of exhalation and excretion. Ideologies are excretions of the mind; they are the exhausted remains of once living ideas. They too must be put safely to the side as toxic wastes that can kill if they are inappropriately taken in as if they were still life-giving food. For Rusty Schweickart, looking down on the violent Middle East, the movement into space became a shift from the ideologies of "us and them" to the ecology of consciousness in which opposites are understood in an involvement of "each in all." The furthest development of industrial technology and its extension into space brings about a classic enantiodromia as technology triggers a mystical change in consciousness in which an *object* becomes a *presence*. But it also brings about a cultural condition in which the spiritual unconscious, or Gaia, is precipitated into consciousness.

As Bateson has shown, most of Mind is, and must be by definition, inaccessible to consciousness,[11] but how we designate the unconscious is part of the history of consciousness, part of that image in the rearview mirror that tells us where we have been. Looking back over the twentieth century, we can now see that the uncovering of the unconscious has moved through four stages. First came the uncovering of the instinctive unconscious with Freud; this was essentially a revelation of *eros* and *thanatos* in the basic animal life. Then came the uncovering of the psychic unconscious, the collective unconscious, through the work of Jung. This was a revelation of the archetypes of the emotional life of the soul. Then came the uncovering of the intellectual unconscious, the "positive unconscious" in the work of Lévi-Strauss and Foucault. For the structural anthropologist, mythologies and the sexual life of preliterate humanity expressed patterns that were invisible to the savage but perceived by the ethnologist. For the cultural historian of civilization, like Foucault, the *episteme* of an age was the hidden structure of the mind, the intellectual unconscious that held economics, linguistics, and art in a relationship not seen by the people of their own era.[12] Bateson's analysis of the ecology of Mind is the transition from the uncovering of the intellectual unconscious to the precipitation of the spiritual unconscious. This revelation takes two forms: first, the unconscious becomes experienced as the body not identified with and hitherto seen as "the other," namely, the environment; and second, the environmentally compressed social consciousness integrates under the threat of crisis to precipitate, not a literate civilization, but a collective consciousness. Another word for revelation is apocalypse. This mythic narrative of the end of the world should not be taken literally, but should be recognized as expressing not annihilation but the ending of a single world-system.

Catastrophe literally means "turning over." When one turns over compost with a shovel, one is indeed creating a catastrophe for the anaerobic bacteria in the pile. Wars can be the turning over of civilizations, but for humans with a more ecological awareness, the transition from civilization to planetary culture could be more subtle, unimaginable, and so gradual that, though sensitive individuals in various ages intuit the transition and express it in art and also paranoid utterance, the transition itself, the turning over, does not take place in time until it is finished. Perhaps the transition from civilization to planetary culture is like the transition from Paleolithic to Neolithic, and the artists who sensed the passing of their era said farewell to it in Lascaux and Altamira. For the artist, nothing is the same; for the common man, nothing has changed, Perhaps this is what Yeats meant when he said, "All life is waiting for an event that never happens."

And yet something happened to Rusty Schweickart, and something happened to our world when we saw it from space. Perhaps there is a logarithmic progression to the rate of change. What a few intuited at the time of Hieronymus Bosch became more widely seen as the discontinuity between the rate of change and the rate of adaptation became more dramatically widespread in the century of the Wars of Religion. Certainly with the rapid death of the forests and vineyards in Europe, and with overpopulated Mexico becoming to the United States in the twentieth century what Ireland was to England in the nineteenth, the world does seem to be a place where culture and ecology are disastrously maladapted to one another.

The samsaric creatures who distort the process of adaptation with conscious purpose do not seem to know what they are doing. When the West Germans created the "economic miracle," they did not know that they were killing the forests. When the city fathers of Los Angeles connived with General Motors to eliminate the Pacific Electric public train system in order to build the freeways, they thought they were making something called "progress." This mistake seems to be as old as civilization itself. In ancient Uruk, Gilgamesh and Enkidu thought that the right way to go out and make a name for themselves was to slay the spirit of the forest. Whether it makes DDT, plutonium, thalidomide, and dioxin, or genetically engineers a bacterium with which to spray fruit trees in order to retard the damage to agribusiness from frost, or inserts an insect gene in corn, civilized humanity will continue to make progress and profits in this unmindful way.

Conscious purpose derives from conscious identity. As this Western industrial civilization of ours reaches its grand climactic finale, it is timely for us to look back and ask ourselves: Who is this "we"? What is this story we keep telling ourselves about *Western* science, and *Western* technology, and *Western* humanistic values?

The narrative of identity in which we take our being as members of Western civilization marks time with various monuments and builds its pantheons to celebrate the heroes of the nation. But if we move our eyes up from the level of the streets of Paris or London, we do not see people or their monuments any longer. The samsaric creatures who thought that they were separate from nature when they dug wells and chopped down trees do not show up in the Landsat picture, except at the end of the story, in the changing colors of a polluted Mediterranean. As we look down on the ecological stage of Western history, we see a mold called civilization spread from river to sea to ocean. We do not see tribes, peoples, or nations, but we do see four distinct ecologies affected by human culture. I prefer to call these configurations "cultural-ecologies," rather than nations or empires, and I look back at the narrative of "Western civilization" to see it as a cumulative movement through four cultural-ecologies.

The first cultural-ecology of the West was the Riverine, that lattice of city-states spread between the Tigris and the Euphrates in the fourth millennium B.C.E. This historic transformation of Neolithic villages and towns into cities was not simply an expression of an increase in population, but involved a reorganization of the structure of society. This systematic transformation involved new forms of communication in the appearance of writing, new forms of technology in the appearance of plows and irrigation works, and new institutions in the forms of standing armies and elevated temples. We now look back in identification with this complex and call it "civilization" to see ourselves in it.

Neolithic gathering and gardening were attuned to local conditions and limits. There were no great irrigation systems to transform the marshes of gatherers into the fields of farmers. Civilization, by contrast, involved an extensive alteration of the landscape, and the dikes and canals of the irrigation works contributed greatly to the salinization of the soil.

The salinization of the soil is civilization's first form of pollution, and it tells us right at the start something important about the structural organization of civilization: pollution is not a random noise or static that clings to the transmission of the signal as consciousness passes through the medium of nature, but rather it is itself a communication, albeit an unconscious one. It is not random, but a systematic description of the form of the disruption; it is like a shadow that describes the form of an object's intruding into the light. It is not noise precisely because it is a signal; but because it is not recognized to be information, it cannot be classed as an ordinary signal. So let us call it dissonance rather than noise, for dissonance derives from cultural conventions of tuning. Dissonance can contribute to background noise as long as it remains unconscious and unrecognized, but if the dissonance becomes interesting enough to attract awareness, and thus is pulled out of the unconscious into the creative play of mind, then it becomes recognized as a signal.

Pollution, like a neurotic symptom, is a form of communication. To ignore the symptom, to thrust it to the side of awareness and push it back into the collective unconscious, is to perform the same action that created the pollution, the dissonance, the neurotic symptom, in the first place. Ignoring the communication stimulates it to the point that the dissonance becomes so loud that it drowns out all other signals. Ultimately, the ignored and unconscious precipitates itself as the ultimate shadow of civilization, annihilation. This is another way of expressing the adage: "If you do not create your destiny, you will have your fate inflicted upon you."[13] The creation of destiny depends on maintaining a more permeable membrane between noise and information, unconscious and conscious, nature and culture.

Civilization, however, is not surrounded by a light, permeable membrane, but by a wall, and the intensification of consciousness through writing only contributes to the ignored accumulations of the unconscious. The salinization of the soil was not seen or heard. A local technology, defined by the city's limits, created a problem area larger than its political area of control. And so the very attempt at control through irrigation only created a larger area of the uncontrollable. It would seem that nature has its own homeostatic mechanisms of order that use disorder, and any cultural attempt to control an area rationally only seems to generate a shadow that has the ability to eat the form until it disappears in the light. We call nature "wild" with good reason, but the fascinating aspect of the cultural patterning of urban civilization is that the problem or crisis, the dissonance, can itself be read as the signal of emergence of the next level of historical order.

It can, that is, be read as a signal by the historian, because what may be unconscious for a society is information for the historian, precisely because he or she is not *in* that society's time. So it is that one culture's noise and dissonance can be the succeeding culture's information.

The Mediterranean cultural-ecology followed the Riverine. In the expansion of city-state to empire, political areas strained to become coextensive with their resource areas, if not their ecosystems. In urban civilization a center-periphery dynamic was established in which power was at the center with the literate elite, but the resources were at the periphery with the illiterate provincials. Soil loss at the center could be offset by importing foodstuffs and materials from the periphery. But as the extension of empire from river to sea took place, deforestation was the price paid for creating large fleets.

Soil loss can be seen to be a local problem remedied by importing food, but deforestation is not simply the removal of an object; it results in an alteration of the climate over a large area. Here again we see the pattern that the appearance of a crisis can be read, not simply as noise picked up by the signal in transmission through a medium, but as the signal of emergence of the next level of historical order. Removal of a forest creates an atmospheric disturbance. And here again we see that as the area of conscious control is extended, the area of unconscious unmanageability also expands. The human crisis comes as a result of the fact that the political area and the ecosystem are not coextensive. (By definition, conscious purpose and the larger "ecology of Mind" can never be congruent.) Nature has built-in defenses against rationalization, because total management would shut down spontaneity, novelty, and change; therefore the defense is a tissue of contradictions. Disorder is homeostatic; the capacity for innovation is held through forms of maintenance that involve noise, randomness, and catastrophes used as stochastic mechanisms. The shape of nature is a form for which we have no topological mapping. It is a form of opposites: order and disorder, steady state and catastrophe, pattern and randomness, continuity and innovation. The ultimate enantiomorphic polity is Gaia herself.

The third cultural-ecology is oceanic, specifically Atlantic. We know this formation under the more familiar designation of "industrial civilization." The technology is one of steam and internal combustion, and this gaseous, thermodynamic activity is poetically appropriate,[14] for the environmental disturbance it causes is not merely one of soil loss or local deforestation, but of global atmospheric change. These are the changes that we who come at the end of industrial civilization can see in the forms of acid rain and the Greenhouse Effect. Once again, the political area is not coextensive with the ecosystem, though the British certainly strained to make it so in the nineteenth century; and once again we can see that the crisis indicates the emergence of the next level of historical order, for the atmospheric damage indicates a movement in cultural activity from the oceanic to the planetary.

The fourth cultural-ecology is space, first the aerospace of World Wars I and II, then the space of interplanetary exploration; the human economic focus for this cultural shift from industrial to postindustrial is the Pacific Basin. In the postwar cultural relationships between Japan and California, one can observe the technological shift from matter to information in the emergence of the electronic industries that now shape the new economy. The old European civilization spread out from London and Paris to New York; the new Pacific Basin civilization spreads out from Los Angeles and Seattle to Tokyo, Sydney, and Shanghai.

Although this new culture is focused on the Pacific Basin, the fourth cultural-ecology has a global quality in that it is affected by an accumulation of all the preceding crises. We encounter salinization and soil loss in the United States from the use of center-pivot irrigation and the mining of fossil water, sudden and massive deforestation in Latin America and Indonesia, atmospheric changes from industrial pollution, and alterations of global weather patterns. Whether all of these forms of pollution will result in the advent of a new ice age, or the melting of the ice caps and the flooding of coastal cities such as New York, or both in succession, is now being debated by scientists.

When we look back over the pattern of development from Riverine to Mediterranean to Atlantic to Pacific-Aerospace, we can see that Western civilization is correct in having identified itself with the Sumerian urban revolution of the fourth millennium B.C.E. The story of the rise of urban civilization is our story, and not one of the environmental problems of civilization has been "solved" since 3500 B.C.E. The problems have simply been deferred by moving into a new cultural-ecology. But now we have come full circle, and all the problems are accumulating in what can only be described as the climax of civilization itself. The human response to this climactic crisis has been Janus-headed; one face looks for a way out through an imagination of the past, the other through an imagination of the future. The celebrators of hunting and gathering as an ecologically balanced culture, such as the poet Gary Snyder, tend to see civilization as a pathology. The celebrators of technology, such as the physicist Gerard O'Neill, saw nature as the wrong vehicle for culture and proposed space colonies as the proper medium in which technology could grow independent of the constraints of an earthly ecology. Both of these reactions to the present are literally reactionary. Hunters and gatherers are not innocent, and the extinction of the Pleistocene megafauna can be blamed on their techniques of using prairie fires and stampedes to eliminate whole species in their hunts. Civilization, if it is pathological, simply makes the underlying pathology of human culture more visible. The task is not to eliminate humanity in a romantic celebration of nature, or to eliminate nature in a romantic celebration of technology, but to understand the enantiomorphic dynamism of that oxymoron *human nature.* The planetary ecological crisis allows us to see the nature of a planetary ecology for the first time. If we can begin to understand the pattern that connects noise to innovation, catastrophe to selection, nature to culture, we have the possibility of becoming alive in vitally more imaginative ways than in the male-bonded clubbiness of the hunting camp or the space colony.

Since the beginning of civilization, there have been wild slippages in nature that have always kept it out of the control of culture. Heisenberg's Indeterminacy Principle is not simply a narrative limited to quantum mechanics; it is a narrative of the limits of the mappings of observation: if you can fix a society's location, you cannot fix its ecological momentum. Bateson saw the discrepancy between conscious purpose and the larger pathways outside the body in the ecology of Mind as a form of disharmony that resulted in crises of maladaptation; but perhaps the relationship is more basic than that, more a question of ontology than epistemology. Perhaps knowing can never become identical with *being*, or perhaps it can only become so with the achievement of Buddhist Enlightenment.

The Christian poet Robert Browning wrote, "A man's reach should exceed his grasp, else what's a heaven for?" Since we have no historical evidence of the presence of Enlightened societies—even the Taoist monks contributed to deforestation by using charcoal to make the ink with which they made their celebrated paintings of nature[15]—we can assume that the slippage of nature out of humanity's grasp has to do with a fundamental slippage of being from knowing. Like a shadow that does not permit us to jump over it, but moves with us to maintain its proper distance, pollution is nature's answer to culture. When we have learned to recycle pollution into potent information, we will have passed over completely into the new cultural-ecology.

Although nature has her built-in protections against imperial schemes of total control that would, in effect, be totalitarian, human beings cannot refrain from the impulse to extend their control. Each time that Western civilization expanded, it struggled to internalize the preceding cultural-ecology, and it strained its reach to extend its grasp in a political control up to the margins of the new cultural-ecology. Mediterranean culture internalized the Riverine, and Roman society strained to turn the Mediterranean area into an empire. The English internalized the Mediterranean (that is what Nelson's Column celebrates) and strained to turn their new oceanic cultural-ecology into the British Empire.

The idea of empire may be compelling for some people, but as Bishop Berkeley said in rejecting scientific materialism, "We Irish think otherwise." The idea of empire is a poor abstraction of a living process; it is a crude oversimplification of an ecology, and perhaps this is why life always defeats empire in time. The historian of the modem world-system, Immanuel Wallerstein, sees the expansion of the West as an ambivalence, even an oscillation, in the application of two forms of political activity. One he characterizes as that of a world empire, the other that of a world economy.[16] The past struggles between the United

States of America and the Soviet Union could be seen, therefore, as not so much a conflict between capitalism and communism (the contents of their structures), but between a modernizing and deracinating world economy that puts McDonald's hamburgers in Paris and Disneyland in Tokyo, and a traditional and very conservative form of world empire that sought to define the periphery in terms of the single center of Moscow.

One can thus say that an empire is an abstraction of an ecosystem, that an economy is a shadow form of an ecology, and that what human beings are now struggling to create is a healthier cultural-ecology in which pollution, noise, and dissonance are understood and structurally integrated in the design of new forms of human settlements.

The United States has a high tolerance for noise, but is actually a fairly homogeneous culture; Western Europe has a lower tolerance for noise, but is highly heterogeneous. The double presence of noise and heterogeneity made it impossible for the Soviet Union to swallow up Western Europe. The imperial way of dealing with noise and dissonance is simply to suppress them. The economic way of dealing with them is to circulate them through society and make a profit from the movement across thresholds. One cultural system places a high value on stability and sees the steady state as the natural condition; the other places a high value on innovation and sees change as the natural condition. Europe was the unstable shore between the world economy of the Americans and the world empire of the Russians, and its instability still makes it rather unpredictable, especially in Eastern Europe and the Balkans. But its very instability showed that it was no more open to conquest by the Russians than Latin America was to conquest by the gringos. America's fear of Soviet expansion was a projection that was a caricature of its own military expansion into Puerto Rico and Hawaii. Reagan's fear of the Evil Empire and communist world domination was Manifest Destiny in a Hollywood projection in which the reversed image is righted by the lens that has cleverly hidden the inversion of reality.

The season of cultural florescence is, by its very nature, transitory. The Dutch were world leaders in commerce, art, and

science in the seventeenth century, and in the Glorious Revolution they served to establish the economic infrastructure and
institutions that paved the way for the rise of England in the
eighteenth century. The English, in their turn, invested in the
United States and then saw their role of world leadership pass
to the Americans in the twentieth century. In the 1980s, some
Europeans, such as Johan Galtung and Jacques Attali, predicted
that the Americans would lose their leadership to the Japanese.
Americans, for their part, were afraid that the twenty-first century could see Japanese momentum added to Chinese mass to
create an unstoppable Asian velocity in the future. But in truth,
the Americans were happy to have the Japanese to compete with
in the race for the supercomputer, for Americans need a Super
Bowl to spur them on. The Japanese never were likely to over-
take the Americans, for their primary and secondary educational
systems tend to crush the young and kill any sense of risk taking, imagination, spontaneity, and play. American high schools,
by contrast, are a joke, but as kids tinker with computers, as
once they tinkered with customizing cars, they are free to grow
in the more relaxed ways that lead to such mythic stories as the
creation of Apple Computer and Microsoft. Easy high schools
and encouraging universities are the secret of American success.
Given its Stanfords, Cal Techs, MITs, Berkeleys, Swarthmores,
and Pomonas, America is not yet into decline, but is, in fact,
entering a period of cultural transformation greater even than
the Industrial Revolution that passed over Great Britain in the
eighteenth century.

　　If we were simply shifting the center of world-power from
one world-city to another, "history" would be the same old
story of rise and fall, but because we are moving out of one
cultural-ecology into another, history is unpredictable, but not
unimaginable. The larger patterns of historical development can
often help us to see what is forming "local" events, much in the
same way that geology can help us to see what forces formed our
local hills and streams. One way to reimagine history is through
a pattern-recognition that attends to the manner in which different philosophies of history become isomorphic. The four

cultural-ecologies that I have chosen line up in an interesting way with the typologies of both Marx and McLuhan. One focused on systems of production and distribution, the other on systems of communication; but the shift from one form to another was synchronous with a reorganization of cultural-ecologies, as we can see in the following table:

Cultural-Ecology	Economy	Communication System
Riverine	Asiatic	Script
Mediterranean (Transcontinental)	Feudal	Alphabetic
Atlantic (Oceanic)	Capitalistic	Print
Pacific-Aerospace (Biospheric)	Socialistic	Electronic

Because Marx was writing in the middle of the Industrial Revolution, he overemphasized technology and the means of production, for, in large measure, he was also reacting to what he felt was the excessive idealism of the Hegelian school. Marx had no way of anticipating the shift from hardware to software, and he had little chance to see that capitalism's emphasis on innovation would carry it from one culture into another—and that Russia's revolution would lock its grip onto the industrial mentality. McLuhan lived in the middle of the shift from print to electronics, and he had the advantage of the perspective that comes from sitting to the side of history. Marx lived in the center of the industrial mentality in London; McLuhan, however, was not in Los Angeles, but Toronto, and Toronto, like a fly in amber, is a beautiful fossil of the Scot's vision of the Protestant ethic and the spirit of capitalism. A devout Catholic, McLuhan disliked change and innovation, but in his fascination with the culture he studied, he spoke for the ambivalence of most Ontarians. Nevertheless, McLuhan saw what most Americans could not, and that was themselves. His analyses of the television culture of the sixties make even more sense when extended to the Internet culture of the present.

As we consider the pattern that connects Marx's means of production to McLuhan's system of communication, we can see that each shift from one to the other tended to introduce a new form of polity:

Cultural-Ecology	Polity
Riverine	City-state
Mediterranean	Empire
Atlantic	Industrial nation-state
Pacific-Aerospace	Noetic

Because the eighteenth-century Industrial Revolution turned technology into a form of idolatry, most contemporary political scientists tend to see only technology and economics as expressions of political reality. Pure science, art, and any form of spirituality that is not religiously institutional are not taken seriously. Fortunately, the French have made up for the Comtian positivism that they foisted on the world, for now cultural historians such as Foucault and Serres look beyond technology for the implicit configuration—the syntax of thought—that is common to the narratives of myth and science. Now, finally, postindustrial humanity is beginning to realize that in spite of Lévi-Strauss, we never can have a science of myth (since our being is always more than our knowing), but we will always have changing myths of science.

Foucault introduced the concept of *episteme* as the hidden system of coherence in the positive unconscious of an era. Michel Serres has looked at the origins of geometry and noticed the mythic patterns that unite literature and science.[17] Following these insights, and relating them to my own previous discussions of the narratives common to myth and science, I would like to propose a further elaboration of the fourfold typology of cultural-ecologies to consider: (1) the dominant form of mathematical articulation; (2) the climactic literary masterpiece; and (3) the dominant mode of religious experience.

Let us begin with the forms of mathematical articulation. Because I am mathematically illiterate, I see patterns precisely

because I am outside the content. Like an illiterate peasant
who yet has some skill in painting complex patterns on pottery, and who, when he comes upon Sanskrit, Chinese, Arabic,
or Greek for the first time, *sees* them as patterns of identity, I
look at mathematics as a cultural description. In each of the
four cultural-ecologies, the processes that have absorbed attention have been quite distinct. It is definitely not the case that
there is one universal human nature with four different cultural
styles of asking the same questions about the eternal verities.
The pattern I see is the following:

Cultural-Ecology	Mathematical Mode
Riverine	Enumeration
Mediterranean	Geometrizing
Atlantic	Notations of movement, dynamics
Pacific-Aerospace	Catastrophe theory-chaos dynamics
	(My hunch is that processual, multi-dimensional morphologies will lead to a return of hieroglyphic thinking of a new sort: a turn on the spiral to a new form of mythic, concrete Egyptian science, not Greek demythologized abstraction.)

The beginning of mathematics, according to Whitehead, was
in the recognition of set and periodicity. The first hunter who
observed that three fish and three bears were both instances of
threeness experienced the observation of sets. The first midwife
who noted the periodic return of the full moon and marked it
on her calendrical stick took the first step toward culturally in-
stitutionalizing periodicity. Elsewhere I have argued at greater
length that these first observations of periodicity had to have
been involved with the menstrual cycle and that the primordial
mathematician was probably not a hunter but a gatherer. The
Paleolithic stick of computation, christened *le baton de com-
mandement* by the Abbé Breuil, was probably no such masculine

extension, but rather a midwife's tally stick for the lunar calendar of "women's mysteries."[18] Menstruation and mensuration are related, and the lunar cosmologies that Alexander Thom has shown to be expressed in the megalithic stone circles of Britain speak of a cosmology that is not military, masculine, or Bronze Age.[19]

The observation of periodicity in Woman and Moon establishes a mentality that becomes developed in the Paleolithic systems of knowledge in midwifery and some form of lunar astrology. But enumeration is not simply counting; it is relating one thing to another. Therefore the recital of the relationships of humans and animals, of offspring and parents, is a form of relating humans to a cosmology. Relating genealogy is relating the individual to the class, and it is so important and valued a form of organizing the universe that the mentality of enumeration survives up into the historic period. The enumeration of all the *me*'s taken by the goddess Inanna from Eridu to Erech is one of the earliest recorded performances of this mentality, but it is so basic that it survives from the Riverine up into the foundations of the Mediterranean epoch. In the catalogue of the ships in Book Two of the *Iliad*, in the recital of the shades who come forth to speak with Odysseus in Book Eleven of the *Odyssey*, and in the recital of the lineages of the gods in Hesiod's *Theogony*, we have three classical performances of the worldview implicitly organized by the Arithmetic Mentality of enumeration.

To appreciate just what a transformation of worldview it is to move from enumerating to geometrizing, we have only to compare the mentality of Hesiod with that of Pythagoras or Plato. Enumeration is a fairly straightforward way of relating humanity to divinity, but when the line folds into triangles and squares, the pattern of relationship becomes more complex. One can begin to see the unconscious emergence of the geometrizing mentality in the *Iliad*, for there the lines of descent are beginning to cross over to create patterns. Leda and Tyndareus give birth to the twins Castor and Clytaemnestra; Leda and Zeus give birth to the twins Helen and Pollux. Then the two sets of twins cross, and Castor and Pollux are raised up into heaven, but Clytaemnestra and Helen remain on earth to become the sources of *eros* and *thanatos* in the world of passionate conflict. When, from another line of descent from Zeus, through Tantalus and Atreus, the brothers Agamemnon and Menelaus are wed to Clytaemnestra and Helen respectively, the lines of descent create the outlines of the battlefield of Troy.

When the line becomes the outline of a form, the metaphor that begins to obsess the ancient imagination is the wall, for the wall is the line seen as container. The *Gilgamesh Epic* opens and closes with a celebration of the wall of the city of Uruk. Book Twelve of the *Iliad* focuses on the wall the Greeks build to protect their invading ships. The wall is the limit, but when Patroclus dares to go beyond the limit, when he dares to go beyond the limits of his own identity by putting on the armor of Achilles, he is cut down. With the concept of the mortal limit, the mentality of enumeration begins to pass over into the mentality of timeless geometry, for the limit is the form of a thing's existence in time as well as space. In the first thirty-three lines of Book Twelve, Homer explores the idea of the wall as a limit of the Greeks' presence in Troy, the limit of the length of time of Achilles's anger, and the limit of duration against entropy. The forces of chaos raging at the edges of order are personified by the gods Poseidon and Apollo, who take counsel together on how to destroy the wall through the eroding force of rivers. But it is clear that what is being described through gods and immortal spirits of rivers are the ideas of entropy and order. A genius such as Homer, possessed by his *daimon,* maintains a permeable membrane between unconscious and conscious, and his ideas have such power because they are neither unconscious nor overrationalized. In that vibrant state they provide vital material for thought for generations to come. When Thucydides portrays the Athenian fleet of Alcibiades proudly sailing off to disaster at Syracuse, he is performing the idea of Patroclus donning the armor of Achilles to go beyond the limit to his destruction; and when Anaximander explores the idea of the edge of things, the wall of definition that separates the limited from the nonlimited, he too is making explicit what was poetically expressed by Homer in Book Twelve:

The Non-Limited is the original material of existing things; further, the source from which things derive their existence is also that to which they return at their destruction, according to necessity; for they give justice and make reparation to one another for their injustice, according to the arrangement of Time.[20]

The wall is the archetypal image of the limit, the edge between life and death, civilization and savagery, and the poetic metaphor of the wall marks the transition in the cultural evolution of consciousness from the mentality of enumerating to geometrizing. In the Babylonian creation myth, the *Enuma Elish* (circa 1000 B.C.E.), Ea puts a magic circle around the younger gods to protect them from the god of the underground water, Apsu. The older gods are rest-loving, but the younger gods throw noisy parties, and so the Great Mother of the salt waters wishes to destroy them so that she may return to her primordial repose. The thermodynamic activity of the youthful and newly emergent gods disturbs the condition of stasis and entropy preferred by the Great Mother, and so the battle of the male god, Marduk, is no longer the old Neolithic cosmology of the male as the symbol of vanishing and the female as the symbol of continuity; it is a battle of form versus entropy, of civilized, military patriarchy versus prehistoric matristic culture, of the enduring and the changeless versus transformation. All the ideas that we have since rearticulated into the Second Law of Thermodynamics have their origin in this matrix of myth.

The *Enuma Elish* and the *Iliad* are profound milestones in the cultural evolution of consciousness, for they sum up and complete an ancient mentality at the same time that they announce the new mentality to come. In Hesiod's *Theogony* and in Homer's *Iliad*, the mentality of enumeration is consummated and finished. Homer brings us up to the edge of the geometrizing mentality, but it will be the work of Pythagoras and Plato to transform mythology into mathematics. And although F. M. Cornford taught us to see that transformation as the great rational leap "From Religion to Philosophy," we now can see what a mixed blessing abstraction is. Homer remains the greater genius, for he understood and expressed the violations of order in a way that no subsequent writer has surpassed.

Throughout the Mediterranean epoch, this geometrizing mentality is dominant, both in its medieval Christian elaborations and in its Islamic variations that replace carnal iconography with abstract geometry. Perhaps the supreme expression of this geometrizing worldview is in the circles of Dante's *Paradiso,* for at that peak of ecstatic visionary elaboration, Mediterranean humanity can go no further. The revolution for modern humanity will be to clear the landscape by calling all into doubt, and Descartes will sweep his mind clean of medieval geometries to create the grid against which to perceive Galileo's failing bodies.

From analytic geometry to calculus, the genius of modern humanity is focused, not on the static objects held in the geometry of a Platonic ideal realm, but on the dynamics of movement. Plato's circles become Kepler's ellipses. Motion, the narrative that was so inconceivable for Zeno, becomes the beloved of Galileo, Kepler, Leibniz, and Newton. For a few centuries, the notations of movement focus on billiard balls traversing a black space; but in the nineteenth century movement becomes generalized into process, and both thermodynamics and evolution extend the mentality into transformations.

Transformations, of course, bring one to the edge of the conventional world of three dimensions, and as the narratives of quantum mechanics flirt with objects of perception that can never be seen but only imagined, human beings begin to realize that there is more to consciousness than objects of perception held in three dimensions. Contemporary String Theory takes this multidimensional imagination even further.

The end of modernism comes with the multidimensional topologies of mathematics and physics. At first, this finish to modernism is elitist and experienced by only a few scientists and artists such as Poincaré and Kupka, Picasso and Einstein, but the rise of electronic forms of communication in our generation has democratized this change of mentality.

With the ability to express multidimensional geometries through computer graphics, electronic technologies are beginning to stimulate the processes of visual thinking. There was only so much one could do with chalkboard and chalk, or pencil and paper, but now combinations of music and computer graphics begin to permit new forms of play with multidimensional topologies and ancient yantras. As these forms begin to dance in the imagination, they conspire against materialism by whispering in the scientist's ear, "All this is disguised autobiography, for these crystals are the intelligible bodies of angels and the soul." Like the slave in Plato's *Meno,* who could reason geometrically because of anamnesis, postmodern humans discover mysteries of consciousness where they least expect them.

Even so groping a comparison of mathematical modes of articulation and literary modes of narrative shows us that Lord Snow's famous remark about there being "two cultures"—the sciences and the humanities—is not helpful in understanding history. Mathematics is relating; genealogy is the logic of one's relations, and both are performances of narrative.

Narrative itself is a human response to time, for it is an attempt to escape the infinity of the present as duration by reifying time into a past. *Existing* means "standing out," "arising out of the indeterminate," or "setting up." Consciousness without an object, without either a sensory construction or a spatial-temporal horizon, would be so maddeningly disorienting as to constitute a condition of absolute terror. Our response to this terror would be to project immediately a spatial-temporal horizon, to project a world.

Something like this consciousness without an object happens every night in dreamless sleep, but since the ego is not there to get in the way with its interpretation of terror, the experience is not remembered. Upon slipping out of this state of undifferentiated Being (described in the *Upanishads* as returning to Brahman), consciousness gathers like a dust cloud collecting in density, and dreams begin to project the sensory/imaginal world of psyche, that shore between the ocean of Being and the island of the ego. Consciousness becomes so enamored with these projections that its attention becomes fixed, and it wakes up into the projection. First consciousness fixes itself in the psychic world, then it falls asleep and dreams what are memories of the psychic experiences, and then it wakes up into the world of the ego to remember the dreams that themselves are memories of psychic experiences. If consciousness were to move without a transition from the fixed attention of the ego to the undifferentiated Being, it would be interpreted as an experience of terror, a death. But this kind of conscious dying, this mystic death, is precisely what the practitioners of meditation strive for. "I die daily," Saint Paul said. But the experience of conscious dying is not exclusively a Christian crucifixion, for students of zazen are awakened at four in the morning so that meditation can begin to wear away the membrane between sleeping and waking. As one is awake in one's dreams and dreaming while meditating, the background to consciousness becomes the foreground as all horizons drop and the ground becomes an open space.

Existence is literally a setup, and so our mathematical and literary narratives are repetition-compulsions that move back and forth across the threshold of the infinitely extended present. We do the same thing when we scratch an itch or make love: back and forth across the sensitive spot, touching and withdrawing, to enjoy the sense of difference that is, as Bateson told us, the experience of information. Narratives leave the present to touch the present, to explain it, to know it. And whether the narratives say f=ma, or e=mc^2, or "In the beginning was the Word," they go back and forth across the erotic threshold that separates eternity and time.

And so narratives are not merely *about* time, they are performances of time: incarnations in miniature that seek literally to re-mind us. As the bard performs his story, so the mind performs its story, the ego. Since the tongue cannot taste itself and the being cannot know itself, we must come at things through reflection and indirection. We tell stories, but the stories are not always directly about what they tell. Hesiod's *Theogony*, that great climactic work of the Arithmetic Mentality of enumeration, is about the evolution of Mind, from the indeterminate, through the psychic realm of gods, and down to the most limited incarnation, the shepherd poet himself.

All narratives, whether they are artistic, religious, or scientific, are at their deepest level disguised autobiographies of the human race. At the level of the root idea, the *Enuma Elish* and the Second Law of Thermodynamics are mythopoeic. Images are generated through a process of deep contemplative attunement to the creative silences of the realm of the Imagination; and so whether we say that the noisy gods protected themselves from the threat of Tiamat through the power of a magic circle, or we say that in the deep thermal vents where life evolved, the amphipathic lipid micels protected themselves from dissolution in the salt waters of the all-surrounding sea through the power of a cellular membrane, we are constructing a narrative in which both myth and science are performances of the Imagination. When science seeks to answer the really big questions by telling us who we are, where we come from, and where we are going—as Darwin and Freud tried to do—science becomes inescapably mythic.

Literature and mathematics both take their root ideas from myth, but because literature performs the root idea in a personified way, in which the planets, seas, and rivers are experienced as spirits, it is a democratization of myth. Mathematics is a mystery school for initiates only, but literature is open even to children. If we look back over the four cultural-ecologies, we can see that for each of these epochs, a particular literary masterpiece sums up the adaptation of consciousness to the ecology of a time and space.

As an adaptation to an ecology, literature behaves ecologically in more ways than one. Like a forest moving through the stages of succession to climax, literature unfolds through three stages of succession: (1) formative, (2) dominant, and (3) climactic. The formative work enters into a new ecological niche of consciousness, the dominant work stabilizes the mentality, and the climactic work finishes it.

The formative work for the Riverine cultural-ecology is the Sumerian cycle of poems on the courtship of Inanna and

Dumuzi.[21] In this love cycle one can still see the historical horizon of the transition from agricultural village to town, for many of the poems are really work songs that maidens could sing teasingly to men as they would beat the churn up and down to make butter.[22] Other poems are competitions between the shepherd and the farmer for the goddess's favors, but all of the poems are clear celebrations of the new agricultural ways of life that were formative of civilization.

The dominant work of the Riverine is the Akkadian poem "Inanna's Descent into the Nether World," a poem in which civilization is expressed, not in work songs for the churning of butter or celebrations of the shepherd over the farmer, but in priestcraft. The "Descent" is no villager's poem, but a highly complex investigation into the cosmological dimensions of the planetary balance between order and chaos, civilization and savagery, earth and the heavens.

The climactic work for the Riverine cultural-ecology is the great *Gilgamesh Epic*. Climactic works, like formative ones, are Janus-headed and face in two directions: they sum up and finish a worldview and also point prophetically to a world to come. In its meditation on death and the slaying of the spirit of the forest, the *Gilgamesh Epic* was prophetic in its study of deforestation, the civilized alienation of the ego, and the limits of masculine military power. All of these themes were to become characteristic of the tragic history of human experience in the succeeding Mediterranean epoch.

The formative works of the Mediterranean cultural-ecology are the Homeric epics. The *Odyssey* quite directly sets up the horizons of the Mediterranean landscape in the voyages of Odysseus, but also establishes the basic theme of the alienation of human consciousness from its source, and the yawning gulf that separates male from female, location from home. The epic forms an archetypal pattern that is to dominate literature for millennia. Contemporary works as different as James Joyce's *Ulysses* and Nicholas Roeg's *The Man Who Fell to Earth* are but modern material cut from the ancient pattern.

The *Iliad,* which seems to me much older and more archaic

in tone than the *Odyssey,* is the primary work that establishes the worldview of order and entropy, consciousness and violence, history and vanishing. So formative is this particular work that I feel that the roots of philosophy and science are here in this *whole* work and not in the more recognized fragments of the Pre-Socratics.

The dominant masterpiece of the Mediterranean is the *Oresteia,* for it expresses what is to be the enduring structure of Western culture: the displacement of relationship by abstraction. Instructed by a male god of light, Apollo, the son kills the mother, displaces the rule of ancient Mediterranean custom, and moves out of the tribe into the polis in a celebration of patriarchy, law, and rationality. For the geometrizing mentality of the Greeks, the entire world becomes reorganized, not in the kinship systems enumerated by Hesiod, but in the new mentality of abstraction in which the chorus distances itself from the *skene* at the same time that culture separates itself from nature in the *polis.*

The climactic work of the Mediterranean, one that completely finishes the mentality as only literature of great genius can, is Dante's *Divine Comedy.* The ancient Mediterranean goddess, who had been displaced from the earth, is now set up in the heavens, and Orestes's *polis* is transformed into Dante's *ecclesia:* the law courts of Athens become the *Candida Rosa* of the *Paradiso.* Reason, which had slain the mother of nature through abstraction, is now wed to consciousness through "the love that moves the sun and other stars." The geometrizing mentality, which had initiated a process of distancing from nature, now finds its true ideal realm in heaven. *Ratio* becomes sublimated into *intellectus,* and the souls of alienated humanity gather in the petals of the White Rose. Pattern flowers.

The formative work for the Atlantic cultural-ecology, one that shows the shift from medievalism to modernism, is Cervantes's *Don Quixote,* a work that for quite different reasons both McLuhan and Foucault chose as the exemplar of cultural transformation. Inspired by a fantastic literature, the equivalent of the communications media of our day, the solitary knight of the sad countenance rides forth in pursuit of a lost culture. Precisely when the traditional culture is about to break up, when the universal ecclesia is about to be replaced by a universal economy, and when the aristocrat on his horse is about to be replaced by the capitalist, the last knight rides forth.

But Don Quixote is not so much a man of the past as of the future. The individual alone with his fantasies, fantasies that alter his very perception of reality, is not a man of the medieval or the classical world. He is the first modern man whose worldview has been transformed, not by parents or priests, but by the media. Precisely because modernism is a wrenching away of the solitary individual from the traditional community, madness becomes the concern of the new age of the mind. Whether we are gazing at the paintings of Bosch, or hearing the cry of Lear on the heath, or watching Don Quixote wear a barber's bowl and call it Mambrino's helmet, we are trying to come to terms with the manner in which the mind creates reality for itself.

The rise of the individual with the new definitions of selfhood is quintessentially a modern phenomenon, and such a cultural appearance is marked by the appearance of new literary genres, such as autobiography. At the formative stage of emergence from tradition, the solitary individual might feel the pull of madness as the way in which the individual could create a personal cultural envelopment. But as the mind begins to grow confident of itself and begins, with Leibniz, to celebrate reason as sufficient to understand and control nature, being, very capitalistically, begins to sell its soul for knowing. Knowing begins to eliminate being, creating the tragic irony that knowing really doesn't know, and in the attempt to control nature, the mind simply becomes the captive of instinctive appetites. The dominant work, therefore, of the Atlantic cultural-ecology is *Faust*. But by *Faust* I do not simply mean the work of Goethe. Lévi-Strauss has argued that every variation of a myth is a performance of the myth and that even Freud's theory of the Oedipus complex is a performance of the myth of Oedipus.[23] In much the same way, the works of Marlowe, Goethe, Spengler, Gounod, and Thomas Mann are all chapters of the larger European work that is *Faust*. Before the West had such creatures as scientists manipulating the genetic code, Renaissance man imagined the alchemist who sold his soul to the devil, and intuited the shape of things to come. In many ways Marlowe's Faust seems to speak to our contemporary situation even more than Goethe's romantic Faust, for Marlowe's man becomes caught up in the banality of power, of fetching tropical fruits in winter or satisfying his lust for control; but the very satisfaction of the desire to control only leads to enslavement. Knowing can never become being; so only the spirit can unmask the covering-over with which the mind bewitched itself.

The climactic work of the Atlantic epoch is *Finnegans Wake.* Coming from a marginal culture at the very edge of Europe, James Joyce very consciously completed Europe. First, he finished the remains of the Mediterranean vision in his *Ulysses,* a work that ends in the affirmation of the feminine brought down out of Dante's heaven and put to bed. Having finished with the voyages of the solitary individual afloat on a stream of consciousness, Joyce went on, in *Finnegans Wake,* to express the transition from print-isolated humanity in its book-lined studies to H.C.E., Here Comes Everybody. At the time when the hardy objects of a once materialistic science disappeared into subatomic particles, so Joycean characters as egos with discrete identities disappeared to become patterns of *corso-ricorso.* History becomes the performance of myth. Characterization is replaced by allusion, and as pattern and configuration become more important than persons, Joyce brings us to the end of the age of individualism. But like Moses on Mount Pisgah gazing into a Promised Land he cannot enter, Joyce brings us to the end of modernism, but he himself cannot pass over into the hieroglyphic thought of the Pacific-Aerospace cultural-ecology to come.

McLuhan considered *Finnegans Wake* to be the prophetic work that pointed to the arrival of electronic, postcivilized humanity, the creature of changing roles who lived "mythically and in depth." Obviously, we are now only in the early days of the transition from the Atlantic cultural-ecology of the European epoch to the Pacific-Aerospace cultural-ecology of the planetary epoch, and no one knows for certain just where these electronic and aerospace technologies are taking us. But since I grew up in Los Angeles, and not in Dublin or Paris, I have a few hunches.

For several reasons, the emergence of the new Pacific-Aerospace cultural-ecology is related to the historical events of World War II. Hiroshima announced the beginnings of the Atomic Age, and the airplane industries of the West Coast were rather quickly transformed into aerospace technologies. With the postwar rise to greatness of Stanford and Berkeley, and with the emergence of Silicon Valley, the Pacific Shift of America from Europe to Japan and China was irresistible.

Perhaps in the next generation or two, a great artist from one of the cultures on the Pacific Rim will create the formative work of art for this new culture, and will do for the Pacific what Homer did long ago for the Mediterranean world. This imagined masterpiece may not be literary, for it is hard to deny that the rise of film, television, and computer graphics have created a new sensibility that cannot be expressed in exclusively literary form. The Homeric epics were popular art forms meant to be recited at social gatherings. We should not fear that new popular art forms mean the death of literary culture. When oral culture encountered writing, literature was created. If literature encounters video discs that have computer animation wed to music, literature will simply reincarnate into a new form; it will not die.

As catastrophe theory evolved into chaos dynamics and continues to evolve into multidimensional topologies, and as film, television, and computer graphics become democratized through personal computers and VCRs, the right hemisphere of the brain is being stimulated by a new form of visual thinking that I prefer to call the return of "hieroglyphic thinking." This designation suggests a new synthesis of art, science, and religion. I may be wrong about the emergence of a new mentality, for there is much in genetic engineering and capitalistic ecology that can force nature and culture into mechanistic forms of control. The future may be an earth that is a space colony *on* earth: a canned civilization of total control and rational management. Since the larger ecology of Mind always eludes the controls of conscious purpose, and since wildness and catastrophes are nature's protection against the forms of rationalization that would make an ecology a closed system, I trust that nature has her Gaian resources to defend herself. If acid rain, the Greenhouse Effect, or other disasters from dioxin or genetic engineering continue to alter the environment drastically, then I believe that the new mentality will finds its *kairos,* its appropriate season of action.

Until such a time of political change or the emergence of an artistic masterpiece that is formative of the new culture, I must make use of what is ready to hand. One experimental work that expressed both a Pacific-Aerospace orientation and visual, mythological thinking was Disney's *Fantasia,* especially his cosmological rendering of Stravinsky's *Rite of Spring.*

All scholarship is disguised autobiography; so I am, no doubt, going back to the fact that I saw *Fantasia* before I knew how to read. For a five-year-old child in 1943, the experience of sitting in a dark cave and watching a vision of the evolution of the earth was a religious experience. No *rite de passage* for an initiate at Lascaux or Eleusis could have been more transporting than that wedding of Bach, Tchaikovsky, and Stravinsky to images of the larger universe. Before, I had known only a neighborhood in a large city, but when I came out of that cave, I knew that I was part of something much bigger, an entire universe.

It is probably for such reasons that I have no Luddite fear of technology, but instead feel that the new developments in computer animation are the beginnings of a new mentality. I look forward to a time when instead of sitting in front of a laptop to create this book, I will be able to sit at a console and compose a video that will have the complex topologies of color, voice-overs, and the music I choose to accompany them, and then be able to email the work to all the subscribers in the satellite network who register interest in the project. We are being told that the age of mass audiences is over and that because there are not that many people out there who care for things as esoteric as ideas, "narrow-casting" is replacing broadcasting; so it seems a waste of trees to try to guess how many people will want to buy the book. Better to have subscribers than customers when it comes to philosophy and *Wissenskunst.* And yet, old capitalistic Disney is there to prove that new art forms need not be elitist. What could be more populist than Disneyland?

In an early study of industrial society entitled *Hard Times,* Dickens contrasted the world of the factory with the world of the circus. The factory was the place of *Homo faber,* but the circus was the place of *Homo ludens*—a place where misfits fit, where the body was revealed, where human beings sported with their ancient companions, the beasts. The circus was the place where feelings and affection could triumph over utilitarian rationality. What Dickens projected as the mirror opposite of Victorian Manchester has, in fact, now become California. The circus may have faded, but its role as a community of play has been taken over by Disneyland and Disney World. And just as the circus was an affront to Victorian seriousness, so the kitsch of Disneyland is an affront to modern sophistication. And yet, there seems to be something occult about Disney's cartoon characters, something almost religious that is at a deeper level of consciousness than intellectual sophistication. The animated figures (recall the Latin root for *anima*-tion) seem to be parodies of archetypes that still appeal to the collective unconscious. In spite of the kitsch, the vulgar sentimentalizations of the past, from animal totemism to Greek paganism, the unconscious is called forth into the space of pop culture. Could it be that the community of the future is not a polis in which abstraction triumphs, but a city of *Homo ludens* in which incarnation itself is recognized to be the ego as video game of the *Daimon?* Perhaps the elitist *Finnegans Wake,* or Ezra Pound's *Cantos,* for that matter, are not that far apart in structure from populist Disneyland, for in all three artifacts many histories and cultures are simultaneously exposed in a single space.

There is, of course, a shadow side to this Pacific world, and the shadow of Walt Disney was Ronald Reagan. Reagan was the man of no identity, only roles, the man who confused both Europe and the East Coast by approaching the presidency not as a task but as a performance. Small wonder that President Mitterand of France, the literary intellectual, found nothing he could relate to in the void of character that was the animatron personality of Reagan.

If Ronald Reagan was the shadow of Walt Disney, the persistent appearance of shadows teaches us not to slip into a utopian futurism in which we imagine that there will be no evil in our hoped-for new culture. There was evil and a dark shadow to the Riverine, Mediterranean, and Atlantic cultural-ecologies, and I suspect that there will be a planetary shadow to a planetary culture.

The problem of evil, as it is affectionately known in the philosophical trade, is a considerable obstruction in the path of futurism, utopianism, or even the larger descriptions of cultural-ecology, for if ideologies are expressions of a false consciousness that prevent people from knowing what they are doing, how can choice—of good or of evil—enter into the patterning of behavior, individual or collective?

If there can be distinct narrative forms to the modes of mathematical articulation for an epoch, as well as for the archetypal literary masterpieces that sum up an era, then there should also be pronounced shifts in the descriptions of religious experience, in the cultural forms of encountering good and evil, as Western Civilization moves from one cultural-ecology into another. Deciding what to look for in science or history is, of course, the first step in the process of discovery.

Re-ligare means "to bind." The religious experience is one that binds part to whole, individual to culture, culture to nature. Knowing is a "fall" from Being in the sense, as Bateson put it, that consciousness only reports on the products of our perceptions. Knowing cannot report on the neurophysiological processes with which those products of knowledge are set up. Consciousness, then, is inherently a limited horizon. The religious impulse tries to reunite knowing with Being. Since consciousness exists in the present, the first religious compulsion is to reunite the present with either a prophetically imagined future or, more often, a past antecedent to the "fall" into consciousness.

Earlier cultures become the metaphor for preconsciousness. Part of the atavistic power of religion comes from its ability to evoke memories of earlier states in the cultural evolution of Mind. In the world of the city, it calls out with the imagery of the farmer; in the world of the farm, it calls out with the imagery of the shepherd; in the world of the herdsman, it calls out with the imagery of the hunt and the cave, or with the imagery of the Great Mother who reigned for the millennia before the herdsman discovered paternity and property in keeping watch over his flocks.

Religious experience is in many ways incredibly reactionary; it does not suffer well the given conditions of any particular present. In the world of civilized and conscious humans, it evokes the ancient collective mind, when consciousness was bound, not by a wall, but by a permeable membrane. And so for civilized humanity, the basic religious experience is to be drawn back in trance, in momentary possession by the ancient goddess or animal spirit.

Julian Jaynes sees the origin of consciousness in the sixth century B.C.E. and claims that before that time the twin hemispheres of the brain were not in communication with one another through the bridge of the corpus callosum. Experiences of the right hemisphere were perceived to be outside the body in voice or vision.[24] This literalist description is fascinating, for it is a scientific form of paranoia, a form of misplaced concreteness that yet in its paranoia intuits something that is going on and that has been missed by normal observers. Scientific fundamentalism, like religious fundamentalism, is always too simple. Jaynes plays with dates to make them fit his chronology, and tries to make the *Gilgamesh Epic* into a work of classical rather than ancient civilization, and his almost phrenological attempt to map locations in the brain with states of consciousness needs to be corrected with the more distributive neurophysiology of Humberto Maturana and Francisco Varela;[25] but Jaynes is on to something, and his original perceptions and theory can be seen as a recognition of the emergence of the hard and discrete ego.

There is a feedback of civilization onto individuation, and

Jaynes is right that Bronze Age changes in burial patterns do indeed spell out changes in the ways of life and not just in the ways of death. In megalithic culture the human bones are placed inside the tumulus in great anonymous heaps. But in the shift from matrilineal to patrilineal, there is a shift in emphasis to warfare and the military hero who wins himself a personal tomb, and a shift to the accumulation of private property in life that is held by sons who can keep watch over their fathers' tombs as the markers of their own dynastic legitimacy.

The ancient Neolithic metaphysic of the male as metaphor of vanishing, as metaphor of the instantaneous temporal modality, is still maintained; but now, on the historical turn of the spiral, the temporality is not associated with just any male who plays the role of the dying god of the dying year; it is associated with a particular male with a particular historical career of conquest. For tribal man, life is a cycle of Nietzsche's Eternal Return; the self is not hard and discrete, and one lives present with one's ancestral dead, or with the animals, with the spirits of place, and with the gods of the sky. Death is no great tragedy, and the funeral is one of the dominant celebrations of life, as it still is in places like Ireland and Mexico.

But with the shift from matrilineal to patrilineal culture, the cycle of the Great Mother is exchanged for the dynastic lines of the Great Father. Private property is won by war and passed on to sons. Religious experience, in this historical context, is to be called back by the goddess to the prehistorical world of the feminine. The linked opposite to accumulation is loss, and so the great problem for male culture, one that is explored in the *Gilgamesh Epic*, is the problem of death. A name is the definition of the ego, but as Gilgamesh and Enkidu go out to make a name for themselves, they discover death. In slaying the spirit of the forest, in cutting down the world of cycles and Eternal Return, they anger the goddess, and she sees to it that Gilgamesh's beloved companion is put to death: not to a male heroic death in battle, but a natural death, that is to say a feminine death, of rotting away in disease and in bed. But the goddess is not able to bring down the whole masculine world, and so Gilgamesh the king survives, and with him his city and its civilization. The poem ends as it began, with a poetic meditation on the hard wall that divides culture from nature.

The hard wall around the city is also the hard armor around the newly emerged self, but this self is a fragile creature that can easily be taken back. Ancient woman as the goddess can easily return from her journey in the underworld beneath civilization to assert her dominance over the processes of life and death. Man will remain the metaphor of vanishing, and dynasties will come and go, but Lilith will always be there to dance in the ruins of male vanities.

Different cultures found different forms of expression to deal with this metaphysic of male vanishing and female continuity. Whether the man as priest puts on woman's dress, or cuts off his genitals and places them on the altar of the Great Mother, or subincises his penis to make it look like a vulva, or has his Orphic head cut off by a gang of women who fling it, still singing, into the collective sea, the structure within the cultural content is still the same: the ego is being annihilated and pulled back atavistically into the collective.

And so for civilized man, the mode of religious experience is momentary possession: momentary possession in sexual intercourse with the goddess (*hieros gamos,* sacred marriage) or momentary possession in a trance communication with the god (*genius loci*).

The Sumerian figure of Dumuzi expresses a cultural pattern that is still close to the Neolithic. Dumuzi as the shepherd-king is raised on high by the goddess Inanna, and then is torn to shreds by her demons when he becomes proud and forgetful of the feminine power that put him on the throne. Dumuzi as the male is still dependent on the female; he is not a military hero who sets up a dynasty to hold onto male power through sons.

When the civilizational process has consolidated its hold on human culture, then the mode of religious experience begins to shift. No longer is one simply drawn back into shamanistic possession by animal spirit or god; now religious experience becomes articulated by a priesthood. Consequently, religious

experience begins to be seen as surrender to authority, as obedience to law. Whether the figure of authority is Pharaoh or Moses,
the pattern is the same: religious value is expressed in obedience
to law.

The archetypal figure of this level of cultural evolution is indeed Moses, the man with the great historic destiny, the man
with the enormous identity. Dumuzi, though proud and forgetful
of Inanna, is not greatly individuated. He is still very close to the
Neolithic anonymity of the vanishing male god; he is only something because of Inanna. But Moses is so great and so completely
individuated that his enormity prevents him from entering the
Promised Land. It is only the truly obedient, routine-operational
manager Joshua who is allowed to take the people into the land
of Israel.

In comparing Hebrew and Sumerian mythologies, we can
begin to appreciate the difference between a formative culture
and a pivotal one within a cultural-ecology. The Sumerians and
the Greeks are formative cultures, the one of Riverine and the
other of Mediterranean. The Hebrews and the Semitic Phoenicians are the pivotal culture in the shift from Riverine into
Mediterranean. Pivotal cultures are reactionary in a positive
sense, for they articulate the past in a way that allows it to be
digested and transcended. The Greeks are the formative force
for what will become natural history, mathematics, and science;
the Hebrews are the reactionary force for what will become the
Abrahamic religions.

The importance of reactionary, pivotal cultures can be seen
today in the case of the Japanese. The Californians are the formative force of the Pacific, but the Japanese are the traditional and
reactionary force. Therefore one should expect that Asian Buddhism will continue to play a great role in the future. Christianity
is reformed Judaism; so the future will probably see some version of reformed Buddhism emerging in the Pacific Rim that will
become the counterbalance to the new technologies, much in the
same way that the Abrahamic religions served as the conservative counterbalance to Western science. At the moment, it would
seem that a Tibetan Buddhism stripped of its medieval culture

and lamaism by no less a global figure than the Dalai Lama himself is the likely candidate, but the even more decultured and ritual-less qualities of Theravada Insight Meditation may carry the day.

The importance of reactionary, pivotal cultures is also seen in the case of the English, for in spite of their eighteenth-century Industrial Revolution, they did not create either the Atlantic or the Pacific-Aerospace cultural ecologies. The Spanish and the Dutch were more formative of the Atlantic, and the Americans of the Pacific; but in their global empire, the British were the great monarchical, reactionary force that struggled to consolidate the world in a vision of a Victorian moral order.

Formative cultures express the creative expansion into new space, whereas pivotal cultures express the consolidation into tradition. The Hebrews are thus concerned with surrender to authority in the obedience to law, but the development of Greek philosophy is to challenge authority and to replace obedience with understanding. For these reasons, I see our conventional designation of the Greeks and Hebrews as the parents of Western Civilization to be correct—though clearly Mesopotamia and Egypt are the grandparents and neither the Greeks nor the Hebrews created what they passed on—but their roles in shaping us are different.

In the social development of religion, priesthood soon becomes priestcraft, and temples degenerate in the Weberian "routinization of charisma" that turns revelation into bureaucracy. But as old religious forms begin to become overripe and rotten, new forms of religious experience begin to emerge in the new civilizational context of intense individuation. Newly equipped with personal identities, individuals are not so ready to submit simply to obedience to law, and so the mental understanding of doctrine becomes more critical than simply identifying with a cultural definition of the group through a religion. The covenant of Jeremiah is not handed down on tablets; it is written in the individual's heart.

The individual prophet is chosen by God, not by the institutions of humans. For a while Samuel tried to interpret his chosenness as the divine foundation of a spiritual dynasty, but as his sons fell and began having intercourse with Canaanitic temple prostitutes, it became clear that sons could not hold spiritual power as sons had held political power before. In the brilliance of the ecology of Mind expressed in the Old Testament, innovation becomes protected as prophecy is randomized, and charisma is protected from routine. Men cannot know which one among them will be chosen by God to become a prophet.

The Old Testament is a pivotal document in the cultural evolution of consciousness in a score of ways. The Near Eastern monarch was a symbol of the body politic and a cultural definition of identity, but the prophetic leaders of the Old Testament discovered that history is a medium through which the mind moves to its destiny with God. It can be said, then, that the discovery of history is part of an interior process of gaining identity through prophetic recognition of one's relation to the culture, the historical movement, and the messianic destiny that waits at the end of history. In effect, the radical innovation of prophecy, in its challenge of institutional priesthoods, is a revolutionary discovery of individuality. Suddenly the power of kingship, wealth, and tribal lineage are put to the side in a psychological definition of value that affirms the power of the individual to embody the presence of God, as the consciousness of history begins to transform history.

Civilizations have parents, and for this civilization we call the West, Greece is the father and Israel is the mother. When Christianity, as reformed Judaism, weds the natural philosophy of the Greeks to the discovery of history by the Hebrew prophets, European civilization is the issue. The pattern is repeated in the Reformation, for when capitalism was wed to Protestantism, industrial civilization was the offspring. And now that reformed Buddhism is being wed to cognitive science, the Pacific Basin is pregnant with a whole new civilization.

Precisely because prophecy is an emphasis on the value of the individual, the individual becomes the space in which the cultural drama takes place. With this new emphasis on the growth of the individual mind, the understanding of doctrine becomes critical. The new *agon* becomes one of prophet against priest, and whether it is a case of Elijah against the prophets of Baal, or Luther against the Pope, the paradigm is the same. When a culture has advanced to the point where private property is mental, then understanding of doctrine challenges the old cultural pattern of Mosaic obedience to law.

For the greater part of the world at this moment, this is as far as humanity has spiritually progressed, and the religious warfare in Afghanistan, India, the Middle East, and Northern Ireland is the old battle of obedience to law versus understanding of doctrine. And if the paramilitary cults of the extreme right in the United States had their way, this religious warfare would be brought home with a vengeance. This old cultural paradigm does not want to die in a peaceful old age, but is bent on putting all the infidels to the sword, and since religion, by its very nature, has a strong atavistic power to pull people back into the ecstatic seizures of the previous level of consciousness, we are not likely to make it into a new Biospheric cultural-ecology without the wars of religion that characterized the beginnings of the Atlantic cultural-ecology. ˙

But since negation is a form of emphasis, the era of religious intolerance, hysteria, and violence will also serve to turn people away from religion in disgust. Religious warfare is now—and most likely will be in the future—one of the cultural forces that pushes people out of religion into a new kind of scientific spirituality (an ethos already expressed by such people as Whitehead and Einstein) that will be to Protestant fundamentalism what Quakerism is to Roman Catholicism. As the mind of religion takes us into cultural entropy by breaking up into smaller and smaller sects, and as the old pattern of the understanding of doctrine degenerates into the violence of schism against schism (one can already see this happening in modern Israel), then perhaps some future prophetic ecologist will arise to say, "The sun is One, but many and different are the flowers it brightens." At that point of religious exhaustion, humanity will pass from ideology, from the stage of the mental definitions of doctrine, to an ecology of consciousness experienced through a universal compassion for all sentient beings. The age of religious conversion will be over, and one will accept a sacred tradition as one accepts a favored poet or composer in an artistic tradition: according to one's inner needs at the moment. Spirituality, like artistic or scientific ability, cannot be dynastic, and parents will find that they cannot pass on their Catholicism, Judaism, or fundamentalism to their children any more than Samuel could pass on his prophetic charisma to his sons.

As Luther, with his heroic individuality, is the archetypal figure of modernism, I imagine that the archetypal figure for the cultural level of universal compassion will be the group, the *sangha,* or the mystical body of Christ. I see popular art forms such as Philip Glass's score for the film *Koyaanisqaatsi,* or Paul Winter's jazz mass *Missa Gaia* as performances of this collective archetype. Architecturally, my own design for the Lindisfarne Chapel in the Sangre de Cristo Mountains of southern Colorado is another invocation of this shift in cultural levels from religion to spirituality.

The most important civilizational force in this cultural evolution from religion to spirituality is Western science. The general public fears that science is a threat to religion and the liberal arts because there are always a few simplistic fundamentalists of scientism, people like B. F. Skinner, Marvin Minsky, and E. O. Wilson, who catch reporters' attention by proclaiming that the mind doesn't exist, or that creativity is a fake and that the brain is a computer made out of meat, or that the humanities can be replaced with a consilient science and that the state can be replaced by sociobiological management. These statements make citizens feel that their days are numbered and that they are about to become subjects, first of scientific research, then of scientific controls. There is much to fear in the social institution of science, for the sick in the United States tend to lose their civil liberties. Indeed this kind of science is what the Inquisition was to Catholicism: a hideous degeneration of a bureaucracy given too much power. If the state does not intervene to give power to mediocrity, science has certain built-in self-correcting mechanisms that keep it healthy, for science is basically a spiritual enterprise. Science is reformed Christianity; it is to Christianity what Christianity is to Judaism, or what Buddhism is to Hinduism: a visionary simplification. Science is totally dependent on a love of the truth and a spirit of fellowship, and if lust for power and careerist ambitions bring about a situation in which scientists start lying to one another, the whole culture immediately falls apart. In religion, priests can debate or even lie to one another about matters of doctrine; but if scientists start lying about the results of their research, the institution goes into shock, and very powerful forces of self-correction are brought into play.

Science can become evil, but so can religion, art, and politics, for anything human can become evil. But what we can see in the cultural movements from one historical level to another is that evil plays a role in the process of manifestation. For each cultural-ecology there is a characteristic good and, by linked opposition, a characteristic evil. If humble piety is the good that enables one to submit to momentary possession by the goddess or the god in *hieros gamos,* or trance, then pride and an arrogant assertion of the self is the evil act that blocks the good. When Dumuzi becomes arrogant enough to sit on the throne while Inanna goes through hell, he displays the classic pride that goeth before a fall.

All of which is familiar enough. What is not familiar is the fact that this evil is the signal of emergence to the next level of historical order. Pride and self-assertion are a necessary part of the movement from momentary possession to the stable identity capable of making a commitment to obedience to law. It would seem that there is an isomorphic relation between evil and environmental pollution, and that in both cases a form of noise or dissonance is a signal of emergence from one level of order to another. Similarly, when priesthoods have stabilized religion in the form of obedience to law, then evil becomes revolt against authority. But this kind of revolt points up the mental development of a new relativism. Clearly, Moses' revolt against Pharaoh is evil in Egypt but good in Israel. And in much the same way, Luther's revolt against the papacy is seen as good by Protestants and evil by Catholics. So the evil of revolt against authority is actually the signal of the shift to the next level—commitment to belief—with its characteristic good of the understanding of doctrine.

For the Atlantic cultural-ecology, the good is seen as the understanding of doctrine, and if you are a follower of the Pope, Jerry Falwell, or the Taliban, that is as far as you wish to go.

If the good is expressed in the "true" doctrine, then the evil is ecstatic escape or transcendence of moralistic definitions. For fundamentalists, the rock music, drugs, and cults of the young are clearly the work of the Devil. From an ecological point of view, the cults and the counterculture are like weeds in a mono-crop field: they are responses to the artificial devastations of industrialization and temporary efforts to rescue the soil as the field moves through succession back to the natural diversity of tall-grass prairie or climax forest.

Good at one level of order becomes evil at another, and evil at one level of order becomes good at another. In the age of mental understanding of doctrine, obedience to law is evil, for it aborts the development of the mind. In an age of universal compassion, understanding of doctrine becomes evil, for it simply sancti-fies murder in religious warfare. But universal compassion is shadowed by what Erich Kahler called "collectivization through terror,"[26] a psychological technique in which the frightened and alienated individual is comforted by terror and gathered back into an ideology in which the ego is annihilated by the collective.

Terror destroys integrity, the wholeness of autonomous uni-ties; but terror is often used to describe mystical or erotic transfiguration. As Rilke put it in the *Duino Elegies,* "Denn das Schöne ist nichts / als des Schrecklichen Anfang" ("But Beauty is nothing but / The beginning of Terror").

Terror is a crushing integration, the eros of rape rather than love. The difficulty arises when we stop to consider that many religious practices are isomorphic to evil acts, for both can work by the logic of inversion. If the normal man eats, the monk fasts; if the normal man accumulates, the monk lives in poverty; if the normal woman makes love and has children, the nun lives in celibacy. For both sanctity and evil, reversal is the pattern. How, then, can one tell the difference?

If evil can be the signal of emergence from one level of religious experience to another, and if pollution can be the signal of the emergence of a new level of historical order, then what, in Bateson's words, is "the difference that makes a difference"? How do we know when it is appropriate to practice an evil action to approach a higher good, as when Moses rejects Pharaoh or Luther rejects the Pope? And how do we recognize that an evil act is simply evil, as when the Israeli terrorists tried to murder all the Arab mayors of the West Bank, or when the Ayatollah tried to eliminate all the Baha'is in Iran by firing squad?

All the most moving and important performances of knowing in our lives are unknowable. How do we know that we love someone? What is the process of recognition by which we determine that we are in love with one person and not another? It seems analogous to aesthetic knowledge—a similar process of recognition is involved in great music. But what is this discrimination that tells us that Bach is greater than heavy metal; that the Cathedral of Chartres is the living body of an angel, but that Notre Dame is a tourists' museum; that Rockefeller Plaza is a public space, but that the Trump Tower is a vulgar piece of Los Angeles stuck into Manhattan?

Aesthetic knowledge is a feeling about knowing; it is a commentary on the processes of perception. Through the functioning of this metalevel of discrimination we recognize that we can be mistaken in our knowing and even, if we have the kind of aesthetic discrimination called wisdom, wrong in our religious experiences, mistaking some psychic experience, vision, or paranoia for knowledge, when in fact it is only an interpretation of intimations. Because all these mysterious moments of knowing, in love or art, are unknowable, the unknowing kind of knowledge brings us closer to Being. Normal knowing and opinions cannot map Being any more than a bucket can sound the sea; but aesthetic knowing is the art of swimming, the graceful presence that realizes you do not have to measure the sea to love it, sail on it, or swim in it.

When knowing becomes conscious of its limitations, and then turns on them to make the limited process into a dance that talks about the relationship between knowing and the unknowable, it performs Being. This is what both Bateson and Heidegger were trying to get at in affirming thinking: thinking Being. It is difficult to think Being in philosophy, and for me Heidegger's *Being and Time* is a monumental failure; but sometimes we learn more in life from failures than from success.

Thinking Being is difficult in philosophy, but it is easier in music, art, and architecture, and, perhaps, in *Wissenskunst*. The map is not the territory, but some maps do help us find our way home; and yet, home is precisely the place where we no longer need maps.

Humanity is not yet at home in this world of Earth; so we still have need of philosophy. And what Bateson's philosophy can teach us about our battles between good and evil is that "the difference that makes a difference" is difference itself. Evil is the destruction of differences; good is the creation of ever-new differences. Differences are vital, and the good emphasizes diversity, individuation, integrity and participation in the universal through the unique. Evil is just who Goethe's Mephistopheles said he was: "The spirit I, that endlessly denies, / And rightly, too; for all that comes to birth / Is fit for overthrow, as nothing worth."

Evil works through collectivization, not individuation, with the unit crushed into the uniform, the mind crushed into a cult. This is the difference that makes a difference between isomorphic groups: between the followers of Rudolf Steiner and Adolf Hitler, between the communities of Findhorn and Rajneeshpuram, between a tall-grass prairie and the animal concentration camp of a feedlot in Kansas.

Because the good works through the unique and not the uniform, it is not possible to standardize it through time. Each moment and historical situation is unique, and so the good repeated in an inappropriate situation can become evil. It takes a mind to know a difference. No catechism or moral standardization can dispense with the need for a mind to know when a situation is good and when it is evil. Abstract justice in one context can become cruelty; liberal kindness in another context can create evil and enormous suffering. The knowledge of the appropriate season of action, the *kairos* (which is surely an ecological metaphor if there ever was one), is universal compassion: universal because it is extended to the entire ecology of all sentient beings, and compassionate because such right mindfulness is tough-minded and not sentimental.

People who lack compassion often have a secret fear of evil within themselves. They try to mask their fear by loudly screaming and pointing the finger at someone else and accusing them as being the instrument of evil. I have had some experience with people of this mentality who were members of paramilitary right-wing extremist groups in the American West, so I recognize the orientation when it manifests in political personalities such as the Ayatollah Khomeini or the Taliban. People who scream about others being possessed by the Devil are generally possessed themselves, and their lack of compassion comes about because they cannot confront the evil inside themselves and are trying to murder it outside by becoming a murderer. Jung was certainly right in his analysis of the shadow. Those who can own their own projections, and can see their own shadows, are certainly the ones who can be more secure and forgiving of others. Humans are very social and plastic creatures, and when put into a certain context, they can be capable of any evil. Only when we have compassion for ourselves, by recognizing the capacity for evil within ourselves as well as in the historical process of manifestation, can we begin to move from ideological hysteria to the ecology of consciousness that the Christians call *agape* and the Buddhists call compassion.

This knowledge of the ontological role of evil has been with us esoterically for some time, but it is difficult for an ordinary ego to deal with it. The ordinary soul wants a simple list of don'ts, not a vision of complexity. However, the knowledge is there in the New Testament, for Judas cannot go out to betray Jesus until Jesus empowers him to do so. Jesus performs a shadow eucharist by giving Judas a sop of bread in wine. Only then can the spirit

of evil take him over so he can betray Jesus to bring about the redemption that requires crucifixion. Milton only half-consciously
recognized this difficult understanding, for in *Paradise Lost* he
associates Lucifer and Christ as the two sides of an unrecognized
Demiurge. When Lucifer is thinking "one step higher makes me
highest," that is when God the Father announces the emanation
of the Son. As Milton explores the nature of evil, it is no accident
that Satan is the tragic hero of the epic and that God the Father
is a pompous dictator. One can feel no compassion for God, but
the increasing degeneration of Satan is tragic.

If Lucifer and Christ are twin forces of manifestation, the
two sides of the Demiurge of creation, then we cannot kill evil
without ourselves becoming evil killers. Our only way out of this
logical dilemma is to love our enemy, which, of course, is exactly
what Jesus told us to do. The fundamentalist, whether Christian
or Islamic, sees devils everywhere and becomes what he or she
hates. The problem that Milton faced in dealing with evil is one
we all face, for we simply cannot function as an ordinary human
being endowed with an ego if we accept evil as part of a cosmic
process. We cannot simply look at Buchenwald and say, "This
is good, for Israel will come out of this." Such a response would
be equivocation and not compassion.

Like a flashlight searching in vain for darkness, and dispelling
it in the act of looking for it, human beings cannot operate with
an ego and come to terms with evil. Our only way of accepting
its ontology is to violently reject it. Our excretions are intimate
and personal, and tell much about what we chose to take in as
food, but the only proper ecological response to excrement is to
keep it away from ourselves. But, to continue the metaphor, if
we push it too far away, it accumulates and becomes a greater
problem; if we remain conscious of its presence and recycle it, it
becomes fertilizer.

Similarly, it would seem, that when we repress evil violently,
we become violent repressors of others; but if evil is known and
kept at its proper distance from us, new life springs up as we
gain compassion.

Today the overwhelming evil is collectivization through terror

in all its forms, from political torture to warfare, from ther-
monuclear terrorizing to a poisoning of the biosphere that is
bringing the whole human race into one deadly toxic dump
called civilization. What is this evil telling us?

If evil announces the next level of historical order, then evil
is expressing the coming planetary culture. Unconsciously, the
world is one, for global pollution spells out a dark integration
that does not honor the rational boundaries of the nation-states.
Thus we see that industrial nation-states in their fullest development have contributed to their own end. Collectivization, then,
must mean that the future is some sort of collective consciousness in which the completely individuated and conscious ego
becomes surrounded by the permeable membrane of an ecology
of Mind and not by the wall of civilization.

Rock festivals in particular, and rock music in general, seem
to express this fascination with collectivization. Since we have
become an electronic society, a society of information, it is not
surprising that the pollution of the new cultural-ecology is noise
and paranoia. Rock music is about the relationship between information and noise, and if the medium is the message, then the
requirement that rock music be loud to the point of physiological damage clearly indicates that noise is the form that creates
the collectivization that does not honor the boundaries of biological integrity. Playing at a concert in Amsterdam, the Irish
rock group U2 was so loud that it registered as an earthquake
on the seismographs at the university.

Interestingly enough, fundamentalist ministers on television,
such as the Reverend Jimmy Swaggart of Baton Rouge, Loui-
siana, who rant and rave about the presence of Satan in rock
music, are recognizing that there is information in what appears to be noise. Reverend Swaggart is like the Puritans of
Cromwell's time who shut down all the theaters in England.
Swaggart even declaims against gospel music, but he reserves
his particularly Amos-like wrath for the abominations of rock.
His interpretation of what he senses is, of course, very much
like the interpretations of the paranoid, a form of misplaced
concreteness; but paranoia often picks up on information the

normal rationalist misses. In many ways, paranoia is a response
to information overload and too much noise; so it forms, along
with rock music, the dissonance or pollution of a cybernetic society. If Don Quixote was the tragic figure of the age of print, a
man whose senses were sent wandering because of the reading
of books, I cannot help but see the Reverend Jimmy Swaggart
as an equally tragic and quixotic figure, for he is driven to become a media figure to declaim against media society; then again,
Amos ranted, yet he was also the first prophet to start writing his
sermons. Nevertheless Amos the shepherd did not reverse urbanization, and I doubt if the electronic evangelicals will be able to
maintain the Reformation culture of what McLuhan called the
"Gutenberg Galaxy" when they are bound by the same cables
and constrained to become what they hate.

The rise of paranoia, from right-wing fulminations against
the world conspiracy of the Trilateral Commission to Lyndon
LaRouche's hatred of the British Secret Service, is an important
signal that the literate, rational *citizen* of the post-Enlightenment
era is being replaced by the *subject* in a shift from identity
through logical definition to identity through participation and
performance. In one form of consciousness, identity is seen
through similar logical predicates; but in paranoia, identity is
seen metaphorically as the *participation mystique* of common
subjects. Looking at the erosion of good pietist values from electronic evangelical broadcasting, and looking at rock festivals, we
can see that democracy is in for some hard times.

The myth of the Antichrist is that the great collectivizer unconsciously prepares for the enantiodromia—the reversal in the
millennium and the mystical body of Christ. The Roman military
engineers built the roads, then the missionaries used them to turn
the Empire into Christendom. There is a good chance that personal computers and modems could make a Swiss-style, direct
participatory democracy more possible, for it is certainly true
that using print technology the frequent referenda are driving
the average Swiss citizen into apathy. A *de facto* representational
republic is the result of the sharing of information through print
in Switzerland; a *de jure* representational republic was the result

of pamphleteering in the United States. However, both could be replaced by new forms of informational integration that are not as collectivizing as TV sermons and rock concerts.

Although Reverend Swaggart would like to get rid of black gospel music and white rock, it is a fact that music is one of the most powerful descriptions of cultural transformation. When folk music moved from the country to the city, popular music emerged as a new cultural phenomenon. From the cotton fields of Leadbelly to the New Orleans of Bunk Johnson, jazz is an aural history that chronicles our American transformation from an agricultural to an industrial society. And from the New Orleans of Bunk Johnson to the Chicago of Bix Beiderbecke and the Harlem of Duke Ellington is another chapter in the diaspora. The transition from industrial to postindustrial can be seen in the breaking up of popular music into an ecology of consciousness of incredible diversity. The range of jazz forms from those of Dizzy Gillespie to John Coltrane and Miles Davis is one expression of a culture in which neither the melodic line nor the production line holds values together any longer. And the evolution from rock-and-roll in the fifties to acid rock in the sixties was another expression that the dominance of the middle class was at an end.

From the eighteenth-century novelist Samuel Richardson to nineteenth-century moralist Samuel Smiles, industrial society saw the intense effort on the part of the lower classes to take on the culture of the middle classes. Even the aristocrat traded in his elegant satin for the somber black of the capitalist. Gone was the medieval diversity of tramp and tinker, artisan and tradesman, aristocrat and soldier; arrived was the uniformity of clerk and banker. The man of wealth was no longer an ostentatious eighteenth-century rake, and the worker was no longer a peasant in rags, but an Ebenezer Scrooge and a Bob Cratchet of Dickens's *A Christmas Carol*. The distance in dress between rich Scrooge and poor Cratchet is not as great as the distance between lord and laborer in preindustrial society. And now, in our truly postindustrial society, punk music and dress are signaling the end of the middle class's ability to dictate styles of taste and decorum to the social order beneath them. Even more, punk dress signaled a sublimation of British class warfare into information. Since political systems are often parodies of ecosystems, we can see in punk dress all the rich signaling of the animal kingdom, for the stylized *agons* of fighting rams are not fatal, and the elaborate horns are not designed for combat as much as epigamic display. And so it is with spiked hair and metal chains. The "structurally unemployed" of Thatcher's monetarist kingdom had their *agon* with the postindustrial managerial class, a class that no longer had need of them whatsoever: not as slaves, not as peasants, and not as proletarians; but what the English working class did was rather imaginative, for they recycled the proletariat and turned it into pure art style, pure information. Noise became potent information in the form of the global fashion and music industries, and it was appropriate that both the Chelsea School of Art and the punks were on the King's Road. With the recent MTV amplification of music and fashion through the new genre of music video, the size of this global industry is staggering. Considering how little the English had to invest in the working class in the form of the dole and how much they had to waste in the arms race and in subsidizing nuclear power stations, British helicopter companies, and the Concorde, the return on the investment of the dole in the post–working class was phenomenal. From records, video, film, magazines, and changing fashions of clothes, one can see that there was a wholly new kind of parasitical clothes designer and media middle class feeding off the actions of the working class beneath it.

Ironically, though the young worked hard to be visible, the members of Thatcher's Parliament could not see that popular singers were captains of industry; as once were the Josiah Wedgewoods and the Cornelius Vanderbilts, so now the Boy Georges and Michael Jacksons. Show-business Reagan, however, was more sophisticated than dowdy Thatcher, for he came from Hollywood and recognized Michael Jackson to be a media figurehead, and so he received Jackson at the White House like a visiting head of state. Indeed Michael Jackson attired in his ceremonial uniform did look like Pinochet.

So if we look without snobbery or Margaret Thatcher's middle-class ignorance at popular music, we can see that it was signaling the emergence of a collective consciousness as the linked opposite to an elitist scientific-cybernetic culture. If music is an expression of the body politic, then perhaps it is telling us something about the possible future of Europe. If the agony of conflicting political nationalisms is turned into the *agon* of competing artistic nationalisms, then the rich diversity of Europe need not generate social chaos but merely *agonic* display. In the transformation of the working class into the artistic class, there is an analogy of the transformation of political nationalism into artistic nationalism in a global ecology of consciousness. When the Turks in West Germany take elements of Middle Eastern music to create a new popular art form for world music—the equivalent of reggae and JuJu music—they become, not underdogs hated by racists, but the darlings of the Berlin clubs. Jazz did much for the acceptance of blacks by whites in the United States, and you have to have a cultural figure like Duke Ellington before you can have a presidential candidate like Jesse Jackson. When Turkish teenagers began break-dancing on the streets of Berlin, they were signaling back to the Bronx that they had got the message and were on their way.

What all the signaling back and forth indicates is that the social complexity and diversity of the Middle Ages has returned, ending the interval of uniformity that started with the Victorians and reached its peak in the age of conformity in the United States of the nineteen-fifties. It would appear that the complexity of planetary culture, however, is even more diverse than that of medieval culture. Its basic pattern seems to be an array of highly energized oppositions: punk teenager and Chelsea pensioner, orange-suited *sanyasins* and white-suited astronauts, rock stars and electronic evangelists, invisible artists such as Thomas Pynchon or Thomas Nagel, the Sprayer of Zurich, and a whole parade of politicians, snake-oil salesmen, transvestites, and yuppies. With the return of the Middle Ages on the turn of the historical spiral, what comes round again is the return of the knight. Gone is the anonymous GI Joe of the industrial era;

returned is the professional soldier, the elitist ranger, and the
SWAT specialist who, like a white blood cell, is trained to flow
through the body politic and take out assassins and terrorists.

Will this postcivilizational complexity, driven by a runaway
capitalism that generates ever new differences, pollution, noise,
cults, and technological innovation, end in a new state? Will it
become an authoritarian state of the Greens, in which individuals are not allowed to have cars and numerous possessions?
Or will this postcivilization simply spawn a universal fascism: a
fascism of the Left in some socialist countries, a fascism of the
right in some capitalist countries, and a fascism of the Greens
in ecologist countries? Or will postcivilization, in a classical
enantiodromia, reverse itself to become the mystical body of
Christ foreshadowed by the demonic body of Satan? That is, in
fact, what McLuhan, the prophet of the electronic global village,
thought:

> Psychic communal integration, made possible by the elec-
> tronic media, could create the universality of consciousness
> foreseen by Dante when he predicted that men would con-
> tinue as no more than broken fragments until they were
> unified into an inclusive consciousness. In a Christian sense,
> this is an interpretation of the mystical body of Christ; and
> Christ, after all, is the ultimate extension of man.[27]

The worldview of humanity in the Atlantic cultural-ecology
was of *objects* separated in space. The worldview of humanity
in the fourth cultural-ecology (whether experienced by astronauts, like Rusty Schweickart, or mystics, like David Spangler)[28]
is of *presences* in an interpenetrating field. How, then, do we live
with this knowledge? If pollution, evil, noise, and paranoia are
expressions of presences that won't go away, how do we deal
with them? The pharmaceutical giant Hoffman-LaRoche, even
after the accident of Seveso, did not become more responsible
with dioxin; it simply hired Mannesmann to take the cannisters
away, and then Mannesmann hired a truck driver to get rid of
them. Neither Hoffman-LaRoche nor Mannesmann wanted to
think about dioxin; so the truck driver was free to take the metal

barrels and stick them in an empty shed in a village in France. And that is typical behavior for industrial *man:* objects are separated by space, and so we can have mansions at one end and deadly poison at the other. The hospital waste the Mafia dumps in New Jersey comes washing up on the fashionable beaches of the Hamptons.

When we realize that pollution is a presence, we have to create only things we can be present with. Dioxin is a poisonous side-product in the creation of ugly herbicides such as Agent Orange, and it should, very simply, never be made. If we make such things as Agent Orange or plutonium, they are simply not going to go away, for there is no way in which to put them. If we force animals into concentration camps in feedlots, we will become sick from the antibiotics with which we inject them: if we force nature into monocrop agribusiness, we will become sprayed by our own pesticides; if we move into genetic engineering we will have genetic pollution; if we develop genetic engineering into evolutionary engineering, we will have evolutionary pollution. Industrial civilization never seems to learn, from DDT or thalidomide, plutonium or dioxin: catastrophe is not an accidental by-product of an otherwise good system of progress and control. Catastrophe is an ecology's response to being treated in an industrial manner—as the recent outbreaks of mad cow and hoof-and-mouth disease in Europe have shown us once again.

Precisely because pollution cannot go away, we must generate only those kinds of pollution we can live with. Precisely because enemies won't go away, for the fundamentalists' process of inciting hate only creates enemies without end, we have no choice but to love our enemies. The enantiomorphic polity of the future must have capitalists and socialists, Israelis and Palestinians, Baha'is and Shi'ites, evangelicals and Episcopalians.

A monocrop of plants does violence to nature, and the pesticides give us Bhopal; a monocrop of culture does violence to human nature and gives us wars and extermination camps. Neither of the industrial operations called Buchenwald or Bhopal were accidents; they were essential descriptions of the industrial

THE FOURFOLD PATTERN

Cultural-ecology	Form of Pollution
I. Riverine	I. Soil loss
II. Mediterranean	II. Deforestation
III. Atlantic	III. Atmospheric pollution
IV. Pacific-Aerospace	IV. Noise, paranoia

Economy (Marx)	Communication System (McLuhan)
I. Asiatic	I. Script
II. Feudal	II. Alphabetic
III. Capitalistic	III. Print
IV. Socialistic	IV. Electronic

Polity	Mathematical Mode
I. City-state	I. Enumerating
II. Empire	II. Geometrizing
III. Industrial nation-state	III. Dynamics of motion
IV. Enantiomorphic, noetic	IV. Catastrophe theory, Chaos dynamics

Archetypal Religious Leader	Religious Mode of Experience
I. Dumuzi	I. Momentary possession
II. Moses	II. Surrender to authority
III. Luther	III. Commitment to belief
IV. Group as an ecology of consciousness	IV. Symbiotic consciousness

Characteristic Good	Characteristic Evil
I. Humble piety	I. Pride, arrogant assertion of self
II. Obedience to law	II. Revolt against authority
III. Understanding of doctrine	III. Ecstatic escape or transcendence
IV. Universal compassion	IV. Collectivization through terror

Climactic Literary Masterpiece	Characteristic Cosmogony
I. Gilgamesh Epic	I. *Enuma Elish*
II. Dante's *Divine Comedy*	II. Hesiod's *Theogony*
III. Joyce's *Finnegans Wake*	III. Darwin's *On the Origin of Species*
IV. Future work?	IV. Disney/Stravinsky, *Fantasia*[29]

mentality, for how we treat a rock or a weed tells us how we will treat a human being in the future. Until we realize that matter is an illusion and that nature is alive, we will not be able to save our own lives from the violence we inflict all around us. If that sounds like Celtic animism, it is.

The world is now an amphictyony of nations, as once Athens and Israel were amphictyonies of tribes. The evolution of amphictyony into polis or nation was a violent one, and looking at the Middle East or India today there is no reason to think that the transition from an amphictyony of nations to an enantiomorphic polity will be peaceful and rational. But if the evil of collectivization through terror is foreshadowing an emergent level of historical order, then there is some hope that humanity may actually make it from one cultural-ecology to the other.

Each cultural-ecology of the past has had its landscape, its form of pollution, its positive unconscious or *episteme* that united literary and mathematical narratives, and its mode of religious experience, with its characteristic way of encountering good and evil. My purpose in composing a historical narrative in which these patterns are put forward is both personal and social. The personal one is to try to understand why as a Californian I longed for a real world of culture in an imagined "back East" or in Europe, yet could not really accept the narrowing of consciousness I found in Los Angeles, New York, Toronto, London, Paris, Bern, or Zurich. Living in California, I imagined Europe; living in Europe, I reimagined California. As T. S. Eliot said, "And the end of all our exploring / Will be to arrive where we started / And know the place for the first time." The social reason is to hope that this rethinking of the narratives of identity for Western Civilization can make a contribution in the movement from *mystique* to *politique* to become a performance of the planetary culture it seeks to describe.

– T w o –

Cultural History and Complex Dynamical Systems

A history curriculum is a miniaturization of one civilization and a transition to the next. The Irish monks of the Dark Ages of Western Europe miniaturized Greco-Roman civilization into the curriculum of the classics and thus established the foundation for what would become the high civilization of medieval Western Europe. And so now it is necessary for us to miniaturize the civilization we are leaving in preparation for the civilization we are about to enter.

Before adults can prepare the young for the future, they have to know where they are in the present. Our historical situation is that we are in the process of shifting from the era of a global industrial economy of territorial nation-states to a planetary cultural-ecology of noetic polities. This shift involves three disorienting meltdowns or disintegrations that can confuse both teacher and student alike.

The first meltdown is the disintegration of the biosphere, more accurately described as an evolutionary and catastrophic restructuring. A new relationship between the global economy and the global ecology is forcing us to understand the intimate relationship between culture and nature in ways that were not obvious to "Industrial Man." As the national currencies of the global economy interact with currents of the biosphere, the Greenhouse Effect transforms global weather patterns, and hundred-year floods become frequent events, as do hurricanes, continental forest fires, and other disasters, and all of these will draw down on the reserves of insurance companies and the emergency funds of even our prosperous American nation-state. When President Bush says that he does not want to wreck the American economy to preserve the environment, he does not understand that the biosphere can wreck the American economy. Republicans think that nature is a country club and do not understand that it is a complex dynamical system with a Gaian mind of its own. The planetary dynamics of this globally turbulent system cannot be modeled or managed by national governments, and the shadow cast by this catastrophe is actually a caricature of the newly emerging planetary cultural-ecology. This meltdown of the traditionally taken-for-granted biosphere is inseparable from the secondary meltdown of the territorial nation-state, which obviously comes with an enormous release of heat.

Throughout the formative centuries of the rise of the modern nation-state—from the Treaty of Westphalia in 1648 to the recent war in Serbia—nationalist leaders have tried to assert that to die for one's country is a matter of honor and personal apotheosis. Statues of war heroes were forms of urban decoration, and nation-states were personified as folk souls, as feminine spirits calling young men to their deadly embrace in a mythologized vision of death and transfiguration. The trenches of the First World War proved this atavistic rite of sacrifice to be the great lie, and the poet Wilfred Owen nailed a stake into the heart of this vampire with his prophetic poem "Dulce et Decorum Est."

The war in Kosovo, the last war of the twentieth century, was the collision between two cultural evolutionary streams. On the one side was Serbia, going against the modernist stream of Western Europe in its invocation of "sacred land" and the holy places of their Serbian folk identity. And on the other side was NATO, with its professional airmen serving as a highly technologized SWAT police force streaming above these Slavic variations on World War II's theme of *Blut und Boden*. The air war involved no pretense about mystical participation in a folk soul; there was only a most unromantic and impersonal executive instrumentation. But on the ground alongside the explosions of the bombs burned the last fires of romantic nationalism with its fireside sagas of folk identity. It was an ancient story of us and them, a mythic narrative that involved a demonization of an Other and an atavistic descent into cruelty, torture, face-to-face murder, and genocide. For NATO, there was an abstract and high-tech conflict in which collateral damage to inexpensive civilians was lamentable but tolerable, while the loss of pilots or expensive American foot soldiers' lives was rejected as a bad investment. Better to degrade "Milosevic's military assets" than to put our own at risk, according to the corporate wisdom of NATO's board of directors.

For the new managerial vision of the Europe of the euro, there must be a civil society with orderly citizens and civil rights. Turks and Germans shall work alongside one another in Germany, as will Arabs and French in France, for prosperity will lift people up to dream new desires in a new purchase on life, and all will be happy at their work in the new global economy managed by the multinational corporations. An ethnic society based on medieval notions of the sacred will not do, especially if it takes us back to the nightmares of *Völkerwanderung* and genocide.

For the NATO airman, patriotism was not required. Aloft in his jet fighter, this technician would die in the line of duty the way a policeman or a fireman would. But "to die for NATO" would be as ridiculous as dying for Con Ed. Indeed the new transnational state of the new world economy, be it Western Europe or the United States, is now a public service utility.

This transnational wave of cultural evolution will not wash over most conservatives and right-wing extremists without evoking violent screams of denial and holy crusades to go against the current of history. The wedding of patriotism and male violence formed patterns of behavior back in the depths of prehistory and prehuman primate bands. In fact it was a stroke of demonic genius on the part of aristocracies and plutocracies to wed their own economic development to patriotism and the mystery religion of folk souls and holy soil, for this enabled them to send the sons of the poor off to die willingly for the protection of the economic interests of the rich. This mystification of identity and blood lust will not disappear in a day or a century, and, most likely, civil wars within civil societies will prolong its vampiric life; but here and there, gradually, in Western Europe and the United States and Canada, a multicultural society will emerge. The third meltdown or restructuring is the meltdown of the human body. John Maynard Smith and Eörs Szathmary have shown that when a new and more complex level of evolution emerges, the older constituent units lose their ability to reproduce as reproductive viability passes to the higher and more complex levels of organization.[1] Today human sperm counts are declining, and we do not see evolution introducing new versions of *Homo sapientissimus* with a bigger brain and a higher forehead. Rather we are witnessing the emergence of complex noetic polities in which humans are clustering in global electronic networks of consciousness. Machines that were once external to us are now becoming intimate architectures of our involvement with other minds, other cultures, other heavenly bodies.

The shadow-form that is prefiguring our transition from one biological state of being to another is disease. The disruption of the biosphere in industrial global warming and the burning of the rain forests is bringing malarial swamps northward, exposing humans to primate viruses from cleared rain forests, and stirring up airborne viruses into the global atmosphere, where they function as disrupters of the immune systems that have served as traditional definers of the fence between self and other, nurture and nature. This global supersaturation of bacteria, viruses, parasites, chemical pollution, and electromagnetic fields of noise and radiation is forcing us out of one adaptive landscape into another. And when genetically manipulated crops and genetically engineered animals are added to this new postindustrial biome, we shall begin to see not merely industrial but evolutionary pollution as well.

This process of change is not occurring at the twenty-eight frames per second of the movies made for the human eye; the phenomenon is not an event like the dropping of the bomb on Hiroshima; it is a transformation, and even then it is a gradual one, more like the hominization of the primates than the industrialization of eighteenth-century England.

The textbooks that teachers provide for students in public and private schools are not truly describing the world
the students inhabit. And certainly the political news on TV
is not informing us about what is really happening on the
cultural-evolutionary scene.

Education has always been about what teachers see in the
rearview mirror. So a patriarchal culture will write a heroic
history as if the story was only about great men and great battles—from Alexander to Caesar to Wellington and Napoleon,
Montgomery and Rommel. When the historians of such a culture expand their horizons to include science and art, they
simply duplicate their heroic narratives and give us Newton
and Beethoven as geniuses fighting against the titanic forces of
darkness and ignorance. Then along comes a revolutionary class
that mocks the narratives of the ruling elite and claims that history is not about individuals but large and impersonal economic
forces. This was the battle between Carlyle and Marx, and like
the battle between dead white males and women of color of
today, the combatants charged forth on scholarly hobby horses
that rocked back and forth in academic ruts but got us nowhere.
Unfortunately, public school systems today are the battlefield in
which the dying ethnicities of the past fight for three-dimensional
space in a scientific world that has already moved beyond into
the eleven dimensions of string theory.[2]

The public school system was a response to the elimination of
the child labor that had been fine for the farm but was not fine for
the factory. It was also a response to the waves of immigration
from the Old World to the New, a response to the democratization of information in print that allowed institutions to do
what once only the family did. The American public school was
intended to take the immigrant child away from the foreign-
accented parent and make him or her American through the use
of the standardized textbooks of a homogenized culture. Now,
thanks to electronic systems of communication and community,
the age of the industrial masses and mass public education is
over. The public school will not disappear but will be incorpo-
rated into a new and more diverse ecology of information that

will include home schooling, charter schools, religious schools, private schools, and educational associations within the World Wide Web. The emergent institution of education is a noetic lattice. This type of "school" is more like an electron than a nucleus: it has an orbit but not a simple location; it travels through the third dimension of extensive space, the fourth dimension of time, the fifth dimension of the intensification of consciousness in the infinitesimal as well as the infinite, and the sixth dimension of transhuman clusters that bring people together in synchronous associations. These noetic lattices are the kind of connectionist architectures that Western Civilization first experienced in the seizure of sacred consciousness that established the networks of cathedrals across medieval Europe.

Since these cultural transformations are not singular historical events, we have to use imagination and think big in order to become aware of them. So let us move up into the eye of a satellite to look down on the immensity of human history to see its organization as six "transformations" embodied in seven "cultural-ecologies."

Transformations

1. Hominization = 4,000,000 to 200,000 B.C.E.
2. Symbolization = 200,000 to 10,000 B.C.E.
3. Agriculturalization = 10,000 B.C.E. to 3500 C.E.
4. Civilization = 3500 B.C.E. to 1500 C.E.
5. Industrialization = 1500 to 1945
6. Planetization = 1945 to present

Cultural-Ecologies

1. Silvan (prehominid evolution of *Ramapithecus*)
2. Savannan/Lacustrean/Coastal (from *Australopithecus* to *Homo erectus*)
3. Glacial (from archaic *Homo sapiens* to modern *Homo sapiens*)

4. Riverine (ancient civilizations)

5. Transcontinental (classical civilizations)

6. Oceanic (modern industrial nation-state societies)

7. Biospheric (planetary noetic polities)

These large-scale transformations of culture can be seen to express evolutionary bifurcations. At each fork in the road, the old adaptive behavior does not disappear, but the new chreod of development opens up a whole new adaptive landscape of possibilities, and as some organisms cross the threshold into this landscape, the whole relationship of organism and environment changes. This relationship between organism and environment is not a simple one in which the environment determines everything. From photosynthesizing anaerobic bacteria in the Protozoic epoch to women gatherers in the early Neolithic period, organisms change the environment and the environment channels their "natural drift"[3] in new directions with new effects.

"Natural drift" is a better term for this dynamic of emergence than "natural selection," because when we say that certain traits are "being selected for," we energize a nineteenth-century kind of narrative in which natural selection is some kind of reified causal agent.[4] Natural drift, by contrast, is a narrative of bifurcations with consequences. What may have been an unplanned and unconscious or random act of making do with what is at hand—such as prehistoric women gathering the grains of the wild cereals of the Iranian foothills of the Zagros Mountains—becomes a bifurcation that cascades into other bifurcations. The collection of grains encouraged storage and then settlement; thus villages, and perhaps even towns, may have preceded agriculture and served to bring about its gradual development, as Jane Jacobs argued a generation ago.[5] As a random or unconscious action or event contributes to a cascade of accumulating differences, the natural history of that structural coupling of organism and environment can bring forth a novel and complex adaptive landscape, and primates and humans, savages and scientists, can find themselves later on down the line of time to be living in very different worlds.[6] A historical narrative can be an affirmation of distinct cultural development without becoming an ideological paean to European capitalism and industrial progress. One can affirm the validity of emergent properties and emergent domains in the articulation of a phenomenology of culture. All cultures are not identical or equal, but the process of emergence is not necessarily one of moral development. One might wish to say that a particular Stone Age culture is good and kind, whereas another technological society is cruel and evil, or the reverse. For moral or spiritual purposes, one might wish to say that the culture of the traditional Hopi was superior to that of Nazi Germany, or to propose that the philosophy of consciousness in Tibetan Buddhism is more advanced than that of the Marxist ideology of the leaders of Communist China. As a cultural historian, I am perfectly willing to make aesthetic and moral judgments and am not content to rest within a postmodernist relativism in which all cultures are equal and alike. Molecules and cells are not the same thing, and bands, empires, industrial nation-states, and noetic polities are not the same thing.

Each of the bifurcations, or transformations, of culture noted above, from stone tools to computers, is not simply a change in technology. A technological innovation is itself deeply embedded in various systems of values and symbols, so a new tool can be brought forth in synchronous emergence with a new form of polity as well as a new form of spirituality. Cultural history, as opposed to the more linear history of technology, is concerned with the complex dynamical system in which biological natural drift, ecological constraints, and systems of communication and social organization all interact in a process of "dependent co-origination."[7]

In response to the writings of Ralph Abraham on mathematics and evolution, I proposed in 1985 that "Western Civilization" could be redescribed as a development that proceeded through four cultural-ecologies: the Riverine, the Mediterranean, the

Atlantic, and the post–World War II aerospace cultural-ecology of the Pacific Rim. Now, as I have suggested in chapter one, I would prefer to redesignate them as the Riverine, the Mediterranean, the Oceanic, and the Biospheric. Each of these cultural-ecologies was characterized by a mathematical and literary mentality that brought forth a new worldview. The Riverine cultural-ecology is what we conventionally know as the ancient civilizations. The Mediterranean cultural-ecology is what we know as the classical civilizations. The Atlantic cultural-ecology was the global projection of European civilization at the time of the shift from medievalism to modernism. And the fourth cultural-ecology is our contemporary world civilization, in which a global economy is struggling to come to terms with a global ecology in some new form of scientific-spiritual noetic polity, a polity that for lack of a better word I call an *ecumene*. I would, therefore, characterize our era as the transition from a global economy to a planetary ecumene, and the curriculum I am proposing in this book is an expression of this philosophy of cultural transformation.

The curriculum that Abraham and I designed for the Ross School in East Hampton, New York, in the 1990s was one in which the mentality fundamental to a cultural-ecology was understood to be at once a literary and mathematical mentality. Our intent with that curriculum was to attend to the cultural bifurcations in which a new mathematical-literary mentality emerged. In response to Abraham's questions about the absence of the algebraic, I have since expanded these mentalities from four to five. These mentalities are:

1. Arithmetic
2. Geometric
3. Algebraic
4. Galilean Dynamical
5. Complex Dynamical

The Arithmetic Mentality is that of prehistory and the ancient civilizations; it is a generative mentality concerned with the problem of how the One becomes many, that is, how in the world's first universal religion the Great Mother gives birth to her offspring and generates difference and time in the form of the male. The architecture for this mentality is the human body, and the ancient statues of the Great Mother are its iconic expression.

The Geometric Mentality is the mentality of the classical civilizations, and its architecture is architecture itself.

The Algebraic Mentality is the mentality of the transcontinental cultural-ecology of the medieval civilizations; its architecture is a celestial code, that is, a shift from the concrete object to an empowering description registered in a numinous script. This shift can be understood to be really a series of shifts: the shift from the aural to the visual in an alphabetic script; the shift from Yahweh appearing directly to Abraham and conversing with him to God sending the angel Gabriel to Mohammed to dictate a sacred scripture; the shift from mathematics understood visually through geometry to mathematics understood as performative operations or "angelic flights." This greater cultural shift from the classical to the medieval mentality is beautifully expressed in medieval calligraphy, both Celtic and Arabic, and is a form of expression in which the visual is culturally retrieved in an embodied but visionary script that is felt to be an angelic epiphany of Neoplatonic "celestial intelligences." Coeval with this emergence of algebra and calligraphy was alchemy and an erotic mysticism that passionately sought to transcend the material world, with its social demands of familial responsibility and arranged marriages. Alchemy, in its Alexandrian origins, was concerned with refining lead into gold, with transcribing the book of nature into hermetic emblems for the sequence of procedures within the alembic; these emblems were a secret code meant for initiates only. Medieval erotic mysticism was also a process of subliming the body into a state beyond the definitions of societal normalcy, one in which the passion lifted the soul from the natural and the concrete into the ecstatic code of the poetic. The passions of Layla and Majnun in Persia, or of Tristan and Isolde in the

West, are archetypal embodiments of this new medieval mentality, and the mysticism of the Cathars in France, the Sufis, and of the Tantric yogis in India are esoteric expressions of a new and radical mentality that is not directed toward a reinforcement of the values of the concrete objects of a mundane existence. Majnun literally wastes away as his poetic corpus grows and his fame as an ecstatic poet spreads among the Arabs.

The Galilean Dynamical Mentality expresses a shift from the transcendental mode of the Algebraic Mentality back to the immanental mode of the movements of material bodies drawn to earth by gravity. It has as its architecture bodies in motion, whether they be planets, cannonballs, or monetary systems of currency. The Galilean Mentality is the dominant mentality of modernism, and its interactions with capitalism and industrial technology brought forth the emergent domain of the new Eurocentric culture that projected itself as a new global civilization. To deny the reality of this Eurocentric globalization is to be caught up in one or another of the various ethnic identities of the nativistic movements that sprang up all over the world, paradoxically, in denial of the reality their insurrections affirmed.

The Complex Dynamical Mentality has emerged only recently. It is not yet widely understood by our waning modernist culture as a whole, but is more the focus of attention for institutes of advanced study, such as the Lindisfarne Association and the Santa Fe Institute in New Mexico.[8] The architecture for this mentality is the system of systems, an emergent metasystem that is concerned with the self-organizing architecture of all possible architectures, life or artificial life. One result that we can anticipate with the emergence of this new mentality is an etherealization of architecture, the emergence of a new "sci-fi" nanotechnology in which physical structures will be used by being "turned on and off" into visible manifestation, much in the way we enter the dark and turn on the lights.

Each of these mentalities, as Marshall McLuhan noted, can also be seen to express forms of communication.

1. Oral
2. Script
3. Alphabetic
4. Print
5. Electronic

Jean Gebser, the German philosopher of the evolution of consciousness, looked at this same historical progression, but saw it in terms of various mutations of the structures of consciousness that unfolded in the following order.[9]

1. Archaic
2. Magical
3. Mythical
4. Mental
5. Integral

And each of these mathematical mentalities and each of McLuhan's forms of communication or Gebser's structures of consciousness can also be seen to constitute various forms of human societal associations:

1. Culture
2. Society
3. Civilization
4. Industrialization
5. Planetization

Traditionally, prehistorians and anthropologists have classified these social organizations according to the materials of the tools and weapons that they produced, from stone to plutonium. What Ralph Abraham and I are proposing is that we define these societies in the terms of complex dynamical systems; in other words, according to the dynamic of their organization, their structure, and not simply according to their material or ideological content.

The three attractors of complex dynamical systems are: (1) the point attractor; (2) the periodic attractor; and (3) the chaotic attractor.

In a point attractor—such as water going down a sink—events are drawn toward a single state-space. For Stone Age cultures, the Great Mother is the basin of attraction to which all things return. This culture is a condition of Nietzsche's myth of eternal return, a historyless condition in which the ancestors and the past are imaginal participants in a clairvoyant eternal present in which death is in life, and life is in death. Until the rise of literate civilizations, this primordial condition was the timeless world of prehistory.

With the shift from hunting and gathering to food-producing societies, human culture reorganized itself as civilization, and this system was structured in the dynamic of a periodic attractor that oscillated between periods of civilization and periods of savagery and dark ages. In the dark ages that followed pulses of civilization, the Elamites overran Ur, the Chichimecs overran Teotihuacán, the Huns overran China, and the Goths overran Rome.

In the fifteenth century C.E., two civilizations attempted to project themselves out from their homelands to the coast of Africa in what was the beginning of a new world economy. One civilization was Ming China; the other was Portugal. Given the superiority of Chinese civilization, we all should be speaking and writing Chinese now, but Ming China retreated from global expansion and withdrew into a highly traditional Geometrical Mentality of center and periphery, celestial court and lowly foreigners, a mentality that was locked into the expression of a medieval economy of emperor and tribute. It was the tiny and then-inferior culture of Western Europe that projected in a new and more complex polycentric system in which Portugal, Spain, England, and the Netherlands contributed and competed. The phase-space of this new dynamic was the New World economy.

Lest we slip into a Whig history of linear progress, we should keep in mind that this new world economy was one of addiction to substances such as gold, silver, tobacco, sugar, alcohol, and opium, and involved enslavement of the captives needed to mine the gold and refine the sugar and rum. Indeed our contemporary world economy of tobacco, alcohol, cocaine, caffeine, cannabis, and heroin is no mere shadow economy, as legislators in the public light would like to pretend. The shadow economy is an intimate part of the entire complex dynamical system of this global chaotic attractor, one that is structured by both conscious and unconscious, affirmed and denied, human activity. Nevertheless in spite of all the wars of the last 500 years, this world-system has not yet reverted to the conditions of a periodic attractor to return to the conditions of savagery and another dark age.

Each of the five cultural organizations of Culture, Society, Civilization, Industrialization, and Planetization can also be seen to be enhanced and reinforced by a matrix of identity:

1. Sanguinal identity
2. Territorial identity
3. Linguistic identity (language and religion)
4. Economic identity (class and nation)
5. Noetic identity (scientific and spiritual)

In hunting and gathering societies, and in nomadic, herding societies, the tribal and territorial matrices overlap. Humanity is now experiencing the release of heat in a phase change because our whole matrix of identity is shifting, from a culture of economic acquisitiveness and patriotic fervor to a new planetary culture in which science and spirituality are the diploid parents of a new matrix of consciousness. The mystical and animistic worldviews that had been obsolesced or violently suppressed in Industrialization and nationalistic modernization are now being retrieved in Planetization. What is patronizingly dismissed by academics and journalistic critics as "New Age" is nevertheless part of the entire complex dynamical system of Planetization.

Religious fundamentalism and right-wing nationalistic terrorist reactions to Planetization are precisely the sort of heat that is also released in these transitions. Like the Inquisition and the Counter-Reformation, which sought to stop and reverse the modernizing forces of the Renaissance and the Reformation, these reactionary explosions can do a lot of damage and hold up cultural transformation for centuries. Whether humanity can move up to a transcultural identity in which science and a new kind of postreligious spirituality can reintroduce the fully individuated consciousness of the person to a multidimensional cosmos is the question of our time. The cultural project of seeking to bring forth this new mentality is certainly what Ralph Abraham and I have been seeking to do in all our books and cultural projects, such as the Lindisfarne Association and the Visual Math Institute.

Each of these societal forms and matrices of identity can also be seen to embody a characteristic mode of human governance:

1. Dominance

2. Authority

3. Justice

4. Representation

5. Participation

In the hominid band the system of association is based on dominance. This form of association has returned as a nativistic reaction to the cultural entropy of the megalopolis in the form of the teenage gang. In society the form of human association is based on authority, matristic or patriarchal. This form of association also has its nativistic return in the figure of the guru or prophet at the head of a cult or sect. Civilization is an effort—through writing, written laws, and literature and philosophy—to achieve a balance between the conflicting powers of military dominance and religious authority in the form of a system of justice. Plato's *Republic* and Sophocles' *Antigone* are cultural documents that capture the conflict of this cultural shift from a warrior society to a literate civilization. The nativistic return of civilization is expressed in the miniaturized city-state of the university, a literate enclave surrounded by the babble of an electronically nonliterate megalopolis.

In national politics the system of association is based on representation, but this parliamentary and literate system of culture breaks down under the informational overload of the electronic media, and can no longer be based on pamphleteering, philosophical books, and reasoned discourse. It becomes a crossing of entertainment, televised sports, and celebrity management in the popular culture of the shared consensual delusion we see expressed in an American presidential campaign.

The Aum Shinrikyu movement in Japan and the right-wing militias in America indicate that the nativistic movement has now moved up from level III to level IV. Cult is trying to become culture. Terrorism is amateur government. Sometimes in the cases of the Mafia in Sicily, the Medellín cartel in Colombia, the IRA in Ireland, the PLO in Israel, or Milosevic in Serbia, terrorism can challenge the nation-state's claim to a monopoly of legitimized violence. In the case of Milosevic, Serbian nativism moved up from the level of amateur government to legislated terror. As the nation-state melts down in the global economy of GATT and NAFTA, the cult is actually declaring war on the nation-state and declaring its own statehood. Ulster, Palestine, Quebec, Chiapas, Bosnia, Kurdistan, and Kosovo are not the only versions of this shift; religious cults such as Aum Shinrikyu and the Aryan Nation can also seek territorial sanctification of their mental state of being. Not surprisingly, in the American West, the United Nations is hated as a new kind of Catholic Church with a new Inquisition fighting the forces of the new Protestant Reformation. In the formative days of the oil industry, local oil wildcatters in Oklahoma and Texas looked upon oil as just another farmer's cash crop to haul off to the market; and so they hated John D. Rockefeller and could not see, much less accept, his creation of the world's first multinational corporation. In the second generation of this conflict, the children of the wildcatters hated the Rockefeller children and saw their donation of land to establish the United Nations in New York, as well as the creation of globalist associations such as the Trilateral Commission and the Council on Foreign Relations, as an un-American conspiracy masquerading as "the New World

Order." When the United Nations or NATO makes a move to become a global police force and usurp from the nation-state the right to legitimacy in the application of military violence, the subnational group in a disuniting nation makes its move toward regional militias that demand their constitutional rights to have weapons—and not just hunting rifles, but automatic rifles as good as those of the national soldiers they intend to fight.

As the politics of representational government is transformed by electronic media into sports and entertainment, in which one is free to vote for whichever of two celebrities is more successful at fund-raising and advertising, traditional civilization melts back down into distorted forms of its earlier stages—into academic subcultures of unpopular and obscurantist postmodern philosophies in universities, into guru cults of charismatic authority in medieval religions, and into teenage gangs of primate dominance.

McLuhan said, "The sloughed-off environment becomes a work of art in the new and invisible environment." The new and invisible environment is the shift from natural selection through the vehicle of the human animal body to evolution by cultural intrusion. As sperm counts begin to drop from industrial pollution, reproduction shifts from the family to medibusiness. Just as agribusiness once appropriated the family farm, so now medibusiness is appropriating the family body. Small wonder that the conservatives in the suburbs shout for "family values." In urban and postmodern culture, however, the heterosexual body is the sloughed-off environment, so it is being pierced, tattooed, painted, sculpted, tucked, designer-drugged, and de-, re-, and trans-gendered. In our retribalized global village, sex as a reproductive way of life has been replaced by sexuality as a consumer lifestyle choice: straight, gay, bi, or kinky. Since sex is no longer the agency of natural selection, sexual swearing has become not words of numinous and forbidden power but punctuation marks in the new public discourse or in the pop music of gangsta rap. "Fuck," "motherfuck," and "bitch" are no longer private expressions of profanity; they are epigamic cries of the male's sociobiological dance of display, a display no longer intended to attract a mate but to attract an agent for the magnification of his life in the media.

In spite of all this public talk of motherfucking, there are no mothers or fucking bodies in these new modes of electronic communication. As we shift to "out-of-the body forms of projection" into cyberspace networks, it is not surprising that the astral plane takes us over as we become possessed by those noetic parasites that older cultures like to call demons. Much of the imagery of the electronic world of computer games and cyberpunk fiction is devoted to "demons and dragons," voodoo and heavy metal comic book cartoons of beasts, monsters, and great-breasted Amazon warriors of the kind we see with Lara Croft of *Tomb Raider* or *Wargasm*. Recall that three of the teenage boys involved in recent shootings in schools had been put on psychoactive drugs that can have psychotic side-effects, and you can begin to appreciate that media, guns, and drugs have transformed the nature of American culture. The postmodern wedding of drugs and cyberspace has brought about the rebirth of the premodern astral plane. As a technological externalization of the astral plane, cyberspace is a collective subconscious, and has its pornographic realms and its terrorist bulletin boards for bomb-building out there waiting to parasitize consciousness.

Paradoxically, our new state of entertainment has placed humanity within an "up or out" evolutionary bind. If the new media continue to be created by the spiritually challenged—game designers and Hollywood producers—they will bring forth a culture of destruction that leads to cultural destruction. These new electronic media that work with the speed of light require a new spiritual consciousness of Light. They are so fantastically efficient that they cannot work to the good unless *we* are good. Who would have thought that these commercial media can only be safely used if we tell the truth and live in the Truth? If we try to abuse and control them for lesser purposes—power, gain, misrepresentation, the accumulation of wealth for private property in cyberspace—then paranoid seizures, cyberterrorism, and a generalized cultural entropy will be brought forth. We end

up in fundamentalist caricatures of religion in the form of demonic states of possession, or in William Gibson's dystopian
nightmares of hypercapitalist corporate disincarnation. Only
now, thanks to cyberspace, these states of possession are not
simply psychic states; they have become virtual states that are
not restricted to Virtual Reality. Unthinkingly, we have raised
the stakes on the nature of thought, for now nothing less than
truth, goodness, and universal compassion are going to get us
through this transition from a global economy to a planetary
ecumene.

Consciousness has now become matter. Small wonder that
the fundamentalist cognitive scientists like Patricia and Paul
Churchland have tried to reduce consciousness to matter in their
doctrine of eliminativism. But they have got it upside down.
Consciousness has become our material reality; as the soil is to
an agricultural society, so is consciousness to ours. Some groups
seek to mine it like coal, and they tend to create the smog in
the noosphere that now surrounds Planet Earth with bad movies
and worse TV. Other groups seek to parasitize it and feed off the
sex and violence like Homeric gods hovering over the odors of
burnt sacrifice. And a few technomystic souls imagine that some
quantum shift is at hand, some sort of superconducting state in
which all the minds "of the Global Brain" will participate in
some transfiguration into a planetary gnosis.

We probably won't have to wait long to find out. The new
electronic media have speeded things up and made the old normalcy of objective reality nonviable. They have pushed us into
this "up or out" scenario, in which we either shift upward to
a new culture of a higher spirituality, turning our electronic
technologies into new cathedrals of light, or slide downward
to darkness and an abyss of cultural entropy where warring religious and scientistic fundamentalisms fight it out in a final war of
each against all.[10] As H. G. Wells warned during the beginning
of this period of Planetization: "The future is a race between
catastrophe and education."

Now that I have placed the education of the young in the
context of our contemporary evolution of consciousness, I hope

it is clear why training people for jobs in postindustrial society, or producing good patriotic citizens ready to die for flag and country, just won't do. To educate a new generation for the new millennium, one has to have an appreciation of the planetary culture that is emerging along with our new global economy. But to be able to *see* that planetary culture, one has to have an understanding of the phenomenology of the development of culture on this planet from the origins of life to the unnamed origin that is now upon us.

– Three –

Cultural History, Homeschooling, and the Evolution of Consciousness

Consider homeschooling to be a trope for the transmission of history from one generation to another. Because a curriculum is a miniaturization of knowledge for the transition from one organization of culture to another, and because we are now moving into a new posthuman organization of culture, the miniaturization of knowledge is an anticipatory movement to our leap forward with a subtle shifting of our weight backward—both to be able to gain balance and to leap farther.

Both the mechanists and the mystics say that we are at a great bifurcation in human evolution. Mechanists like Danny Hillis, Hans Moravec, and Ray Kurzweil prophesy that we are at the end of the human era, that machines are about to be embedded in our bodies until our antique organs of flesh are entirely surrounded by a new silicon noosphere of networked computers.[1] Like ancient mitochondria or chloroplasts surrounded by the gigantic eukaryotic cell, we are about to be engulfed in the next evolutionary stage. So the mechanists see technology surrounding human culture and consciousness.

The mystics, starting with Teilhard de Chardin and Sri Aurobindo in the middle of the twentieth century, also prophesied that we were at a new stage in evolution, but they saw consciousness surrounding technology, compressing and miniaturizing it as an antique fossil of intermediate cultural evolution as we passed on into a posthuman or "Supramental" era in which we were welcomed back into the cosmic play. In the eight intensive dimensions that String Theory claims are infolded into the three

82

dimensions of extension and the single dimension of linear time, we now can see that there is more room for humans to think in than we thought we had during the age of "the conquest of space." For the mechanists, the flesh is slow, sloppy, and wet, and, therefore, primitive. For the Christian mystics, the flesh is the body and blood of the living God. Slow and wet is the ontology of birth and the act of making love. Because the neurons are embedded in an aqueous solution, even distant neurons can participate in a neuronal synchrony through vibrating in the musical harmonies of a single thought. Because the forty Hertz of this neuronal synchrony is slow compared to a silicon computer, it can orchestrate unplanned synchronies in acts of surprise, discovery, analogy, imagination, and metaphoric play. Fast is fine for the programmed, crystalline world of no surprises and no discoveries, but slow is better for the creative world of erotic and intellectual play.

If one speeds up a Beethoven string quartet, one may enhance the baud rate of data processing, but one will no longer have music. In fact, with the increase in speed one has lost consciousness of the work. A Beethoven string quartet is, indeed, a rather sophisticated exploration of the nature of time and consciousness, and the interaction between the different instruments is an artistic recapitulation of the evolutionary development of the nervous system in which different channels of information had to be held over in time and cross-referenced with one another to form an "I." In Beethoven's *Sixteenth Quartet,* the third movement, with the markings of *"Lento assai, e cantante tranquillo"* is so slow as to hover at the very edge of melody and silence. Instead of looking to digital computers as a source for metaphors of mind, it would be more instructive to look, or listen, to music. In Kurzweil's emphasis on speed as the unique excellence of mind, he has lived up too literally to the German meaning of his name. The field of consciousness has more to do with slowness and a higher dimensionality in which hyperspheres, or some other topology, involve simultaneity in a neuronal synchrony in a pattern. A mind, in the opening words of Keats's "Ode on a Grecian Urn," is a "still unravished bride of quietness," a "foster-child of silence and slow time."

Slowness is fundamental to the nature of consciousness, and I would define consciousness as the state-space of the perceptual system. I would argue that in the evolution of consciousness, it was the delay-space between two different channels of sensory registry, say between light and dark, on the one hand, and acid or base—or a glucose gradient—on the other, that enabled the molecularly lingering traces to be cross-referenced with one another in the formation of an interpretative domain, such as "danger!" or "flee!"[2] One channel of sensory registration can be a digital gate, a matter of plus or minus, but when two or three differing sensory registrations are cross-referenced to one another, an emergent domain is brought forth. We move up to a new metalevel, like lines forming the higher dimensionality of a cube or hypercube. An interpretive domain is a subjective experience of a sentient being that can suffer precisely because it has an identity, and is thus, quite literally, identifying with its sensory registrations in an experiential interpretation of its ontological condition, its life. As multiple channels of sensory registration develop, a network develops that stabilizes the delay-space, and this is its nervous system. The natural history of an organism's structural coupling with its environment expresses a reinforcing pattern of response, and this stable response is its identity, its fundamental stabilization of time, its egohood. If these autonomous identities reproduce themselves over time, we call this "evolution."

An engineer can be clever and construct a machine that says "Ouch!" instead of flashing a red light, but this gnostic demiurge is mimicking consciousness to trick humans. The machine is not a sentient being capable of suffering, nor, by imaginative extension and recapitulation of suffering, is it capable of experiencing compassion for the suffering of other sentient beings.

The simple and linear binary gates of 1 and 0 are fine for information processing, but if one wishes to enfold complexity and make it portable for the life of a unique individual, then the sloppy and chaotic folding of proteins in a cell or of neurons in a brain is the way to go. The brain is actually the most complex small structure we know of in the universe. Like the Borgs of "Star Trek," the mechanists have perverted evolution, for it is the wet and the biological that is the truly advanced design, and our clunky computers are the Stone Age idols of our literal-minded American technoculture. So I side with the mystics and think that the mechanists are caught in the boomerism of American hypercapitalism and are simply hawking their wares in order to attract venture capital for their corporate projects.

The evolution of consciousness I have in mind is one in which art, science, and a postreligious spirituality begin to relate to one another in new ways as they explore the eight intensive dimensions of a universe made out of the music of vibrating strings. To understand this change of the state space of human culture, it is helpful to look back and retell the story of human evolution. The curriculum I offer here is meant as an effort in this direction. It is probably too individualistic ever to be adopted in the world of public schools, and, perhaps, is also too radical for the world of private and charter schools. Since I was a homeschooling parent, I like to think of this story as a somewhat shamanic, mind-to-mind transmission of parent to child. Those individuals who are neither parents nor students can think of this curriculum as a rhetorical device for the telling of a story that is appropriate to our cultural evolutionary context.

And as for public schools, I don't foresee them disappearing from the face of the land in a "rapture" in which we are taken up into some new posthistorical state of being. Great waves of immigration to the United States will continue to lift and support our collective societal need for good public schools. Such a need is essential for an open and just democratic society. But at the other end of our pluralistic society, there is another wave of emigration going on in which an electronic American culture is emigrating from the New World to an even Newer World. There are many different reasons to pack up and head out for new territories: drug use in schools, teenage gangs, school violence and cruel hazing, and a mass culture in which art and science are not valued as much as sports, money, and teenage popularity.

The recoil from this mass culture can bounce in opposite directions: on the one hand, we can have a fundamentalist's religious
withdrawal from a secular-humanist, multicultural society, and
on the other, an intellectual's longing to withdraw from a de-
based mass culture to raise children in a more philosophically
and scientifically advanced supraculture.

All of these conditions can cause a parent or a student to
be unhappy with mass society and mass education. Whether for
the scientist wanting to escape the creationism of a school board
taken over by fundamentalists, or for the artist wanting to escape
a school faculty taken over by a postmodernist nihilism in which
all works of genius are nothing but discourses of dominance
and oppression, or for the fundamentalist wanting to escape the
eroticized mass media of consumption, there are many impulses
energizing the search for educational alternatives. All are going
on simultaneously and contributing to the emergence of a new
complex ecology of education in which public, private, and charter schools, Internet schooling, co-housing collaborative efforts
of residents and neighbors, and homeschooling by parents are
all growing at the same time. .

Given the size of public school systems and the social pressure
brought to bear on them, I believe it is unrealistic to think that
they will be the source of educational innovation and cultural
transformation to this Newer World. Public schools will have
all they can handle merely to deal with the waves of immigration and to stabilize safe and modestly academic environments
for their students. It is far more realistic to expect innovation
and transformative learning to come from private schools, charter schools, co-housing efforts, and Internet and homeschooling
alternatives.

The following sketch of a curriculum is aimed at the intellectual elite whose needs cannot be imaginatively met by large
public school systems in which children are persecuted for being
gifted, whether as scientific nerds, poets, or classical musicians.
If someone wishes to use this curriculum as a basis for reforming their charter school or founding a new private school, then
I would advise them to consult with the Ross Institute where

Ralph Abraham and I have tried to address ourselves to the more traditional forms of educational institutions, from kindergarten to grade twelve.

Lest I be accused of being antidemocratic, let me preface my sketch of a curriculum with a sketch of my own educational and socioeconomic background to show "where I am coming from." I was part of the vast postwar movement from the Midwest into Southern California. In 1945 the suburban tracts had not yet been built, there was not sufficient housing for families, and most landlords with apartments did not wish to take in noisy children, so at the age of seven I was packed off to St. Catherine's Catholic military boarding school in Anaheim, a school that was more like an orphanage or prison than your usual upper-class boarding school. I stayed there for two years, summers included, before my parents found a one-bedroom apartment for our family of five, and I was able to live at home and go to a Catholic parochial school.

Neither my mother nor my father was educated beyond the eighth grade, so my socioeconomic background can be described as Irish working class. My mother had been "lace curtain Irish," but she fell from grace and was disowned when she married a divorced Protestant, so the life of my parents in the Depression was anything but middle class. As an Irish Catholic born in Chicago—but whose own mother had been born in Ireland—my mother was raised in what E. R. Dodds has called "a guilt culture."[3] Traditional Ireland was "the land of saints and scholars," and in the revolutionary tradition of "the hedge schools" that defied the Penal Laws of the English, learning was respected, even by the poor. But in moving from the Irish subculture of Chicago to the Latino culture of Los Angeles, my mother did not realize that she was also moving from a "guilt culture" to a "shame culture." In a shame culture, to excel is to threaten the integrity of the group, to cause others to lose honor or self-respect. To appear smart, to identify with the teacher rather than the class of one's peers, is a violation of group integrity. Excellence is only tolerated in sports, for this form of macho demonstration serves to enhance the pride and self-respect of the group. This cultural predicament is also experienced by bright African-American students, for whom doing well in school is considered "acting white."

My mother had tried to do her best to help me by once again trying to send me to a private boarding school in the eighth grade, for just when my older brothers had gone off into the army and navy during the time of the Korean War, my father had collapsed from the incurable disease of scleroderma and had gone off to be cared for in a veterans' hospital. She was also worried about me because two years earlier, I had been diagnosed with leukemia and the doctors told her that I would probably die within a year. The osteopathic doctors she consulted for a second opinion took out my tumor in two operations, told her it was a goiter in the wrong place, and hoped for the best. But a goiter it was not, and the primary tumor in the thyroid was left to produce and distribute its malignant metastases.

The 1940s and '50s was not a healthy time to grow up. There was, as there is today, an idolatrous belief in the invincibility and utopian perfection of technology. I remember waking early to watch the sky light up as Man beat Nature to the punch with the preemptive strike of an early dawn in an open-air nuclear explosion. When the Santa Ana wind blew the dust into the San Gabriel Valley where the cattle grazed, the milk was never destroyed, and Iodine 131 made its merry way through the food chain and into the children's thyroids, much as it did in the Ukraine after Chernobyl. To make matters worse, there were also X-ray machines in all the shoe stores. I remember twinkling my bony toes in the eerie green light. And to make matters even worse for me, I was given X-ray therapy for my tumor, which only made the cancer more malignant.

And then there was smoking. Everyone smoked everywhere. In my family of five, the other four members all smoked in the confining space of our one-bedroom demi-bungalow. Not surprisingly, I developed asthma and had difficulty breathing. So with a sick husband and son, and two children off to war, my mother had a lot to contend with. Since she had to work in an office, and did not want me to be home alone, she sought out yet another military boarding school, Urban Military Academy in Brentwood. For a year I went to this private school, where world history was taught by the Headmaster, a Ph.D. who had taught European history at U.S.C. He insisted on teaching his eighth-grade class as he had in university, and I loved it. It was wonderful to be treated as an adult, and I was fascinated with his more human approach to European history. The nuns in parochial school had certainly never told me that Popes had mistresses and children, or nephews that they would make cardinals at thirteen (my own age at the time). I excelled in the class and became an honor student. But the school was not in central L.A. where I lived, but in wealthy Brentwood. My school friend was the only other bookish student in the class, one who delighted in history and happened to live in a mansion overlooking the Pacific Palisades and had a weekend horse ranch in Santa Barbara.

Invited to be his house guest, I was stunned by the luxury of having a room of my own, by the strangeness of a bathroom with a bidet, by the unreality of being driven to the movies by a chauffeur in a Cadillac limousine, of being driven to a birthday party at Douglas Fairbanks's house, where the Firestone children threw ice cream at the others in a spoiled rich kids' food fight. At dinner in his home, I was disoriented by being served exotic dishes, such as barracuda, on silver platters offered by a butler and a maid. I had never even experienced a middle-class life of having a home, a dining room, or a bedroom of my own, and I certainly knew nothing about the protocol of dressing for dinner, so I showed up in the formal dining room in my playclothes of school T-shirt and chinos—much to the disapproval of my colleague's mother. I continued to annoy her as I developed a fierce attack of hay fever at their horse ranch in Santa Barbara and spent an entire weekend sneezing violently—feeling mortally ashamed, as only thirteen-year-olds can.

My mother had meant well, and had simply not wanted me to be a latchkey kid when she was away at work, but she could not keep up with the costs of the school, even though the headmaster tried to encourage her to pay by informing my classmates, in front of me, that she had not yet paid for my uniforms or the semester's tuition. Her social experiment lasted only one year, and for the ninth grade I returned to a Catholic high school in south central L.A.

At St. Agnes High School that year, when I was fourteen, there was a pretty girl in my history class whom I liked. She responded to me flirtatiously, but also liked to compete with me in class. One day we were given some national machine-scored test in world history. She smiled at me, offering to race me through the course. Stupidly, I responded, and finished the whole test at half-time. When the marks were returned a week or two later, the nun made the mistake of letting the class know that I had gone off the charts, receiving an impossible score higher than the hundredth percentile. I had only missed one question out of 100. The girl was livid, as she saw that she could not come close to competing with me.

Although she had flirted with me, she could not afford the loss of face by associating with the likes of me, and she had already chosen as her boyfriend a Mexican who was head of the Latino teenage gang that ran the school. In her rage, it was a simple matter to aim her boyfriend in my direction in revenge for her loss of face. It became impossible for me to go out to the schoolyard at recess and lunch, and impossible even to continue at that high school. Fourteen-year-olds did not pack Uzis in those days, but they did carry switchblade knives.

At St. Agnes High, I was risking eternal damnation by reading *Candide* in the ninth grade, and risking death by daring to go out into the playground, so I transferred to L.A. High, and although I was terrified to attend a large high school of 2400 students, it was actually a fairly safe if unintellectual school. In the Mc-Carthy era, intellectuals were held in contempt and ridiculed, but not attacked on the playground; it was as if we were untouchable perverts against the natural order of things—teenage popularity, sports, cars, and money. I was often accused of being un-American, communist, and queer, simply (and rather ironically) because I had read Emerson, Thoreau, and Melville on my own and quoted them in class. "Whoso would be a man, must be a nonconformist" and "to be great is to be misunderstood" were among my favorites.

After the hell of St. Agnes High, the purgatory of L.A. High and two more operations for cancer of the thyroid, I went on to the intellectual paradise of Pomona College, where in my senior year, I received a Woodrow Wilson Fellowship for graduate study at Cornell. Though more famous than Pomona, Cornell was actually not as good, managing to conceal a collective mediocrity and snobbish conformism with the camouflage of wealth and Ivy League prestige.

I am offering these personal remarks simply to indicate to other parents that I have experienced the cultural extremes of education in America, and to indicate as well that my commitment to an intellectual elitism comes from an economically deprived person's desire to escape poverty and violence for a world of culture and commitment to excellence.

The curriculum in cultural history that I am offering here is meant to be a spinal column supporting all the other related studies in art, mathematics, and science. I am following the principle that it is better to study the scientific and mathematical idea or operation in the actual historical context in which it emerged, and that it is better to study American history in the context of the world history that brought it forth. And I am also following an idea that I proposed in 1974, and for which more recently Dr. Leon Botstein, president of Bard College in New York, has argued in the aftermath of the shootings at Columbine High School. Dr. Botstein feels that collectivizing teenagers in large groups during the years from sixteen to eighteen is asking for precisely the kind of trouble we have seen, and "that high school is a failure not worth reforming."[4] Sixteen-year-olds, Dr. Botstein argues, belong in the company of adults, where they can be socialized to an adult life through training on the job as apprentices, or, if they are naturally inclined intellectuals, as students in colleges and universities. In my 1974 work, *Passages about Earth: An Exploration of the New Planetary Culture,* I argued that there was a naturally oscillating cycle of periods of *Homo faber* and *Homo ludens,* and that the years from fourteen to twenty-one were definitely under the spell of *Homo ludens.*

> From the ages of seven to fourteen, when they delight in collecting objects and facts, children should be in school; but by the time of their teens they should be released from school, and in good Maoist fashion sent out to work and play in rural communes.[5]

The curriculum I am sketching here does not include a senior year. It stops at age sixteen and recommends that at that point the student should go away to a good liberal arts college, or engage in some experiential program of work and apprenticeship under a mentor other than his parents or former tutors. After receiving my program of homeschooling, my son went to Amherst at age sixteen and graduated with honors four years later. I was able to homeschool my son because I worked at home and could be with him throughout the day. Thanks to personal computers, many parents, and not simply writers, now work at home, so the possibilities for homeschooling have increased.

Even if one is in the privileged position of working at home and can take on the responsibility of homeschooling as a parent, it is still wise to try to work in association with others, either through co-housing or collaborative efforts with friends and colleagues. If suburban parents can get together for Little League, soccer, Campfire Girls and Boy Scouts, then they can also do the same for philosophy and science. But if one is a parent who must leave home to go work at an office or factory, then homeschooling is not a realistic option. Under these circumstances, it would be better to choose private or charter schools if one wishes to have an alternative to the public school system.

Culture is a shared system of values, and no child can be healthily raised in a parentally controlled isolation tank, so play groups, and clubs for activities will need to be arranged to supplement any homeschooling program. If one wishes to escape the competitive and aggressive subculture of sports, then one can substitute group classes in Tai Chi or Aikido, music and dance school, or the wonderful classes that many art museums now offer for children. In our particular case, since we were living in New York, my son and I took advantage of the city, even though in the seventies, New York was at a low point in terms of grime and crime. My son studied Tai Chi in Chinatown, took intermediate recorder lessons in Greenwich Village, studied classical New Testament Greek at the Greek Language Center on 57th Street, and sat in on the lectures on science and philosophy given at Lindisfarne by Gregory Bateson and Francisco Varela. If he felt that he needed a more intense course in science or math, then he took an adult night school course at N.Y.U., where high-school–level courses were offered for adults who did not want the embarrassment of having to go back to an actual high school and sit in class with teenagers. With a resident staff of twenty-four living communally, Lindisfarne functioned as a co-housing experiment, so there were many adults around for my son to interact with as he participated in the work of keeping the communal institute going. For my part, I gave him formal instruction in the research and writing of term papers, took him on research trips, and brought him with me on any public lecture or conference talk that I was asked to give. I reasoned that if a blacksmith's son learned a trade by watching his father, then my son could learn my trade by watching me.

The most important thing in homeschooling is that the parent must spend much more time with the child than a normal working parent does. But the parent must also provide occasions for group play and association with neighbors or neighborhood institutions. If one is raising a child in rural circumstances, then nature itself provides other sorts of opportunities, and on-line courses with museums can help if one is not in a position to take the bus to the Metropolitan Museum. With the resources of the World Wide Web, homeschooling is now much more of a practical alternative than it was a decade ago. Nevertheless the most important element is still the home, and if the parent cannot take the time to be with the child, then the Internet certainly cannot make up for the loss. Many spiritual traditions claim that we take on a body to experience a world of love and compassion. If we lose the body in collective systems and networks of

data processing, we can lose compassion and become intellectually cruel and economically insensitive. We forget that it was
through the body that our child was brought forth, and we forget how to be with another in a sense of presence that enhances
our feeling for the meaning of life. Like "the hungry ghosts" of
Buddhist philosophy, we become wraiths—gray shades whose
lives have been parasitized by computer and cell phone—and do
not realize that they are dead and are only haunting the places
of life. Homeschooling is one way for a parent to move from a
career to a way of life in which the child opens up a new path
to compassionate understanding.

- ℱ o u r -

Homeschooling:
An Outline for a New Curriculum

The curriculum I am offering here is a suggestion for a structured program of homeschooling. It is not intended to be a detailed syllabus of daily and weekly lesson plans, because I assume that the individual parent or teacher will want to do more than follow the Arthur Murray steps on the floor of my dance through history. I am also assuming that if the reader is a parent or a private school director in search of a new approach (such as the Spiral Curriculum I designed for the Ross School in East Hampton, New York), or a public school teacher interested in more than an ideological approach to global narratives of multiculturalism, then a sketch with a slightly different take on cultural history can be suggestive and of service in helping parents, teachers, or even students themselves to enliven and expand their own approach.

The curriculum I am proposing does not think in terms of enculturating students within the patriotisms of nation-states or job-training programs for industrial economies, for that is the role of the public school. Nor does it think of covering the achievements of every culture on the face of the Earth in order to satisfy the identity politics of the culture wars now raging in the universities. That too is the karma of the public school. Instead an evolution of consciousness curriculum tracks emergent states and cultural transformations, and goes to the place of that emergence. As a "thought experiment," imagine how you would report on the human cultural evolution of Earth to a scientific academy on another planet. How would you tell the story to creatures not concerned with the competitive *agons* of

A Curriculum for the Evolution of Consciousness
Three Principles:

1. Match the stages of the child's cognitive evolution to the stages of cultural evolution (Haeckel's "ontogeny recapitulates phylogeny.")

2. Growth is not linear, but pulses in organic stages of *Formative* > *Dominant* > *Climactic* (compare Steiner's Waldorf process of will, feeling, understanding).

3. Present artistic, religious, technological, or scientific innovation in the actual historical context in which it emerged.

ethnic pride and nationalism? A curriculum for the evolution of consciousness curriculum does not think in terms of simplistic splits between culture and nature, but instead envisions cultural-ecologies that unfold as complex dynamical systems in which the traditional divisions of knowledge are inadequate. In what Jean Gebser calls the *Bewusstwerdungs Prozess*[1]—a process of becoming in consciousness—these transformations of culture express a development in which we move through his structures of Archaic, Magical, Mythical, Mental, and Integral both in history and within the soul of the developing child. As I tried to show in my essay on Rapunzel in *Imaginary Landscape*,[2] there is a reflexive nature to children's knowledge, and the fairy tale listened to in rapture in kindergarten can also become the subject for a doctoral dissertation in graduate school.

Because growth does not unfold in simple linear and accretive sequences, this twelve-year curriculum is broken up into pulses of organic growth in three-year sequences. Each triad unfolds in a sequence of *formative, dominant,* and *climactic.* A *formative* movement introduces a new element of consciousness; a *dominant* movement establishes and develops it, and the *climactic* movement consolidates and finishes it. One can think of this dynamic as a simple botanical one of sprouting up, rooting down, and flowering, or visualize it in terms of the four triangular faces of the tetrahedron, the familiar pyramid. The *formative* movement is the base, the foundational platform; the second movement, the *dominant,* is one into a second dimension of the four lines moving vertically in upward growth; and the third movement is one of closure, the closure of the tetrahedron, the *climactic* movement in which one encloses and internalizes that period of growth with insight—symbolically represented by the eye at the top of the pyramid in the familiar emblem of Freemasonry that is on the American one-dollar bill.

In Rudolf Steiner's Waldorf philosophy of education, my pattern of formative, dominant, and climactic corresponds to his triad of will, feeling, and thinking. A formative movement establishes the will, a dominant movement stabilizes it through feeling, and a climactic movement consolidates it through thinking and understanding. The overall pyramidal structure from age four or five to sixteen would look like this:

I. **Archetypal Development:** Stabilization of the physical world.

   Cognitive Development: Stabilization of the child's body and mind.

   Kindergarten (ages four to five): Formative = "The Creation, Vast Elemental Forces."

   First Grade (ages five to six): Dominant = "Patterns of Manifestation in Nature and Art."

   Second Grade (ages six to seven): Climactic = "Coherent World Systems."

II. **Archetypal Development:** Stabilization of the body and the body politic.

   Cognitive Development: Extension of the child's body through instrumentations and development of a sense of balance and justice.

   Third Grade (ages seven to eight): Formative = archaic human forms: the evolutionary development of the human body and of the hunting and gathering band. 2,000,000 to 10,000 B.C.E.

Fourth Grade (ages eight to nine): Dominant = early Neolithic social systems. 10,000 to 3500 B.C.E.

Fifth Grade (ages nine to ten): Climactic = the rise of the Riverine civilizations; the shift from matristic societies to patriarchal civilizations. 3500 B.C.E. to 1450 B.C.E.

III. **Stabilization of the Moral Order.**

Cognitive Development: Development of morality and sense of justice.

Sixth Grade (ages ten to eleven): Formative = prophecy and cultural transformation. 1450 B.C.E. to 350 B.C.E.

Seventh Grade (ages eleven to twelve): Dominant = universal religions and universalizing empires. 350 B.C.E. to 900 C.E.

Eighth Grade (ages twelve to thirteen): Climactic = the climax of hierarchical civilizations. 900 C.E. to 1416 C.E.

IV. **Stabilization of Individual Identity and Rights.**

Cognitive Development: Distancing from family and traditional values in personal identity formation.

Ninth Grade (ages thirteen to fourteen): Formative = modernism and the shift from world religions to a world economy. 1416–1688.

Tenth Grade (ages fourteen to fifteen): Dominant = revolution and the rise of the individual. The philosopher, the scientist, and the artist as the new avatars of culture; the Enlightenment and the Romantic reaction; masculine technology vs. the sacred feminine once again. 1688–1851.

Eleventh Grade (ages fifteen to sixteen): Climactic = global economic consolidation and visionary revolts. Global communications and collective consciousness, planetary culture as expressed in science fact and fiction, and global religious and artistic movements. 1851–2001.

Because mathematics and natural history are subsets of cultural history, I suggest that we overcome C. P. Snow's split between "the two cultures" of the sciences and the humanities by putting mathematics and science back into the cultural context that gave birth to them. Thus arithmetic and number theory should be studied in the context of the rise of the ancient civilizations. Geometry should be studied in the context of the classical civilizations; algebra should be studied in the context of the medieval civilizations; and calculus, chemistry, and physics should be learned in the context of modernization in a historical appreciation of the works of Galileo, Newton, Leibniz, and Boyle. Geology and chemistry should be studied in the context of Hutton and Lavoisier, and evolutionary biology and genetics should be learned in the context of Darwin and Mendel. Ideas about relativity and Cubism should be studied together in a joint consideration of Einstein and Picasso. Adolescents will see all the themes of the curriculum coming together in the hypersphere of the planetization of individual consciousness in the twenty-first century—a time in which the study of consciousness itself becomes the focus of cultural attention in contemporary philosophy and cognitive science.

THE CURRICULUM FROM AGES FIVE TO SIXTEEN

Kindergarten

Theme: The Creation, the vast elemental forces of light and dark, high and low, visible and invisible.

Theory: The reenchantment of animism, reverence for the sacred, for "the suchness of things."

Practice: Lesson plans that are not mediated through abstract instruction, reading, or computer applications; rather, after the insights of Montessori and Steiner, all ideas are implicit within concrete, sensual, kinesthetic and

visionary experience: song, dance, storytelling, play, walks
in the woods and along the shore.

In a Zen sense, very young children are closer to Original Mind.
At origin, we are not so much at the beginning, in a linear sense,
but closer to the source. In *The Language and Thought of the
Child*, Jean Piaget has shown how the worldview of the young
child is one of animism and connectiveness: mountains without
names cannot exist, for there is no sense of an abstract space
in which denatured objects are merely located. Rather than re-
garding this worldview as prescientific or primitive, one should
regard it as a positive "enchantment of the world," one that
healthy adults will need to achieve again in aesthetic modes of
cognitive reverence.

Parents will need to respect this sense of origin by not trying
to force children into becoming little adults by trying to get them
to read as soon as possible or to become disembodied computer
hackers at four years of age. Kindergarten is the time of origin, a
time like Hesiod's *Theogony,* an era of Titanic forces that begin
to bring forth a body within a world. Early childhood is a time
when the spirit exercises its will over the body; disturbed or
abused children, in contrast, disincarnate, and the challenge with
them is to find the right form of loving touch that can convince
them it is safe to take up a fully willed consciousness within
a body.

Early childhood is a time of dyadic elemental forces of light
and dark, up and down, left and right, lightness and heaviness,
little and large, tears and laughter. And so I suggest we begin
at the beginning with creation myths from around the world.
One could begin with a Native American creation myth, then
African or Chinese, and only come to the Bible after one has
heard the creation stories of other cultures. Through song and
dance, clay and crayons, the children can play out the elements
of the stories. An entire week or more of lesson plans could
be devoted to light: light in the morning, light at noon, light
at sunset, light in the rainbow. Science can also be brought in
as another form of reverence for being, for understanding in

awe and amazement at how colors dwell in the rainbow or the crystal. One could look closely at the colors of a candle flame to see how many different sheaths of color one can find there.

Or one can take a hint from the Chinese Zen monk in the *Hua Yen Sutra* who answered a question from the Princess about the meaning of "the jeweled net of Indra" by taking her into a darkened room in which the walls, floor, and ceiling were all mirrors. As he lit a single candle, she saw the individuality of her single flame mirrored to infinity. "Let there be light." But not just the light of one tradition, one Bible, but the bibles of many cultures, and not just the storytelling of religion but the storytelling of science as well.

At the source of origin—in the sense of Gebser's "ever-present origin"—knowledge is integral and not divided into disciplines and technologies. Science and myth, tools and rituals, art and understanding are all together in a cognitive bliss of the sense of the joy, wonder, and fun of being in knowing as a form of being in love—in love with life.

Americans tend to look at kindergarten as mere babysitting, a time you need to get through as fast as possible until you have got the kids up to speed through reading and computer-skills development so they can get down to the real work. This is about as far from the truth as you can get. Actually, what the enlightened adult needs to do is to return to this earlier mind and reachieve it with all the powers that have come from intellectual development. Great scientists and artists have been able to survive their education, but most people have been beaten into submission and have been turned into used and abused tools.

Because I have lived in Switzerland and looked over my wife's shoulder at her work with kindergarten-age children, I have come to appreciate just how wrong the American approach is and why our children have become so violent. From infancy, American children are raised to process the system of neurological interruptions that flicker in rapid parallel lines on the radiating cathode tube of the television set. They then move on to Nintendo and Sony PlayStations. I have heard computer experts on TV insist that as soon as an infant can click a mouse, he or she should be educated with and through a computer. Neither the chairs, keyboards, nor monitors are ergonomically designed for children, but there is more physiological damage going on here than carpal tunnel syndrome.

Swiss educational psychologists, such as Remo Largo and Richard Humm in Zurich, have found that trying to force rapid growth inflicts great physiological and psychological damage. As Largo has said: "You can't make the grass grow faster by pulling it upwards."[3] Each stage of growth must be accepted and affirmed, for it sets down a foundation for higher cognitive skills that will manifest later. For example, in order to develop a healthy coordination of the cerebral hemispheres, infants need to crawl and alternate left and right parts of their bodies in their rhythmic progression forward. If they are blocked in their physiological development by doting parents who carry them everywhere, whether in prams or snugglies, they can later manifest a lack of hemispheric coordination in dyslexia. If doting parents leave the light on in the child's bedroom to protect them from the dark, they can develop nearsightedness later. The circadian rhythms of light and dark and the bilateral rhythms of left and right need to be respected.

From the ages of infancy to five, it is important that the kinesthetic and auditory realms of experience be fostered and not rushed over. Infants need to listen to classical and folk music, to be spoken to in full and complex syntactical sentences. If the mother speaks to the infant in one language and the father speaks in another, then the child will grow up bilingual and will have the neuronal development to acquire languages and accents more easily. If the young child grows up in a culture of music, storytelling, dance, movement, drawing, and painting, then the right hemispheric mode of pattern recognition will be profoundly developed, and this mode can often be the source for imaginative creativity and discovery later at higher levels of cognitive activity in art and science. By forcing young children into the linear, processed world of the alphabet[4] and the digitalized culture of the computer, we are unfortunately indeed preparing children for the world we adults have created.

Americans are so addicted to their digitalized world that I expect that IBM, Microsoft, or the Media Lab of MIT will take over all public school kindergarten curricula to get the kids clicking as soon as possible. Just as "Sesame Street" did not teach kids to read but taught them to like TV—as Neil Postman has pointed out—so will the electronic industry ensure that a new generation grows up liking computers. If they have problems in school, then the American medical industry can step in to fix the problem with drugs for depression, hyperactivity, or attention deficit disorder.[5]

To counteract this culture calls for a culture richer than that of technological idolatry. It calls for parents who spend an inordinate amount of time with their children, touching them, reading to them, playing blocks with them, drawing with them, going for walks with them. Busy yuppie parents don't allow themselves to have this time, so they place their infants in day-care centers within weeks of birth. Our American pattern of technoculture is so deeply embedded in our belief in quick fixes to all problems that we would rather add on a new drug rather than change behavior. If children are hyperactive from a diet of caffeinated soft drinks and sugared cereals, Americans would rather administer another drug like Ritalin rather than change their way of life. Our culture has become so addicted to consumer electronics, guns, and drugs that we could have a dozen Littletons and still carry on in our conviction that the answer to the problem is not a change in culture but a new application of a new technology or technique.

Kindergarten is a Zen-like place and time in the sense that it really involves a kind of "mind to mind transmission" from the teacher to the students. The being and soul of the parent or teacher is more important than his or her pedagogic philosophy. He or she can be Waldorf or Montessori or Piaget, but what truly matters is the sense of soul-presence that embodies knowing and reverence. At the level of facts and information, one could have very little "content," and yet at the level of the context of being with a teacher—being with others, being with knowing—an enormous amount could be going on.

Because knowledge is integral at this early level—as it should be again at the postdoctoral level—there should be no divisions into disciplines such as science, art, religious studies, and languages. Songs can be learned in many different languages. One can play with blocks and learn about forces and balance—pillars and capitals, cantilevers and corbelled arches—and never realize that one is learning about elementary physics. One can play with rhythm and not necessarily know that one is playing with numbers and patterns.

To protect the space for an integral culture, I suggest a very slow process of unfoldment—an inverse logarithmic progression—in which the teacher spends an entire week on a theme. A week or two on creation stories from around the world. A week on light. A week on color. A week on the sun. A week on the moon, the stars, the elements of earth, air, water, and fire.

Only toward the end of the year should we come around to letters and our "ABCs." But here too I would propose that we respect the protohistorical cosmologies out of which these alphabets have emerged. The teacher could study Robert Graves's *White Goddess*[6] to consider the ancient runic alphabet of trees, or read Rabbi Lawrence Kushner's *Book of Letters*[7] to consider the folklore and Kabbalistic magic of each Hebrew letter. In Berkeley, California, Stan Tenen has produced a videotape that shows an even more complex Kabbalistic cosmology and topology that is implicit in the Hebrew letters. He shows how a single topological cross section of a dimpled sphere, when rotated in light, casts a shadow that can produce all the letters of the Hebrew alphabet.[8]

If the ABCs are returned to their source in the magic of origin, the wonder of connectiveness can be appreciated and letters can take on a magic that is easier for a child to appreciate. Teaching the alphabet as an abstract system of arbitrary signs for broken fragments of sound is not a good way to get children to understand the nature of meaning and the meaning of signs. I can actually see spending several weeks with the letters—without any compulsion to form words—before one settles down to the magic of names.

If, as Piaget says, children cannot conceive of a mountain existing without a name, it is not because they are stupid but because they appreciate the primordial power of the name that brings things into being. One could spend an entire week on names: their sacred power, their call to the imagination, the names of the children and their cultural history.

Finally, in an *aria da capo,* at the very end of the year before the summer's holiday, teacher and students could return to the story of the creation and read the first sentence of the Old Testament, "In the beginning God created the heaven and the Earth," or the opening of the Gospel of John, "In the beginning was the Word."

The First Grade

Theme: Patterns.

Theory: Evolution from the animism of presence to persons, personified objects, and musical instruments.

Practice: The exploration of patterns in snowflakes and flowers, rhyming words and songs, patterns in rhythm and dance.

In kindergarten, the student was concerned with transpersonal forces like light and dark, light and heavy, loud and soft, happy and sad. In the first grade the process grows less gaseous and more distinct. The spiral nebula evolves into a distinct solar system. One plays in the sandbox and watches to see at what point the sand hill collapses into a cascade. One puts three blocks together in a cantilever, and then pushes two sets of three blocks together to create an arch to drive a toy car through. One looks to see which flowers have five petals and which have six. One plays with drums and bamboo flutes. Rhyming poetry, traditional children's songs, skip-rope chants, and many different patterns become important.

One old-fashioned technique that has now come back in the idea of Hebbian neuronal development is the virtue of memorization. Committing songs and stories to memory is not a mechanical denial of creativity, as we thought in the sixties; it is actually helping to develop the neuronal pathways of complexity in the brain. In Gerald Edelman's "neuronal Darwinism" of the brain, it is a question of "use it or lose it." Our traditional grandparents who compelled us to learn the Catholic mass in Latin or the Torah in Hebrew knew something that our liberal parents didn't. So let the children commit many poems and songs to memory. Let them begin playing with and studying a foreign language and stay with it for many years.

At this stage of development, the implicate knowledge of kindergarten begins to differentiate into explicit domains. It is not yet a case of conflict and division, say between science and the humanities, but mathematics does begin to exercise a fascination of its own, one that is not opposed to, but is still different from, the fascination of poetry. The Arithmetic Mentality begins to manifest at this stage, and catalogues and lists have a magic of empowerment. Naming all the planets, or all the numbers from one to ten in another language, gives a sense of magical empowerment in and of itself. Knowing the names of the major dinosaurs or the trees in one's local area feels good in and of itself because the act of naming is a performance of a new growth of consciousness.

At the age of six, objects and instruments take on a special power. Tools such as bicycles become extensions of the will, of one's sense of being in a body. Musical instruments and computers can now become possible extensions of mind. But it is not yet musical theory and harmony, but the instrument itself that holds out the fascination of the performance of power in which Self engages the Other.

Reading, writing, and arithmetic, the simple physics of blocks and constructions, the play of patterns in nature, the use of tools and musical instruments, the memorization of songs and stories and poems, the biology of evolution of plants and dinosaurs—the second year (traditionally the first grade) is the cultural shift from creation to creatures, from mystical awe to magical ritual, from the presence of Being to being present.

The Second Grade

Theme: Systems.

Theory: The evolution from creation to creatures to the self instrumentally active in its world.

Practice: The increased use of computers and high-tech externalizations of imagination in taking patterns up to the level of patterns of patterns in systems. The development of group movement and dance into sports and athletic competition in which the performance of self-accomplishment naturally expands at the same time it is channeled into a sense of the group and the team.

By this age, the healthy child is feeling a strong sense of self and an instrumentally enhanced sense of adequacy in his or her world—whether it is simply a case of riding a bicycle around the neighborhood, or hitting a baseball with a bat. This is the appropriate age in which sports and technology come into their own. In both study and play, the dyad of self and instrument, self and team are experienced constantly, so this is a good time to explore the dynamics of object and system. It is also a good time to study the sun and the solar system of the planets, the ocean and the continents in the Gaian system of planetary self-regulation of temperature, the foxes and the hares in May's study of ecosystem regulation, and the flora and fauna of the local ecosystem. With a strongly developed sense of the self enhanced through instrumentalities, this is a wonderful time to encourage what Yeats called "the fascination with what is difficult." From shooting a basket to riding a bike, to playing an instrument, to learning to speak a foreign language with the right accent, to computer skills, this is a time to let kids really take off into what they love. And everybody will love something different, so one should observe and accept how the play group itself becomes an ecosystem of diversity, with one child expressing one gift, and another a quite different gift. Rather than pitting one child against another in a spirit of winner/loser competition, this development provides the group with an occasion to discover how groups can stabilize through diversity, how patterns of systemic self-organization can bring up symbiotic cultures of cooperation and mutual development.

Parallel to this development of self and culture is a development of knowledge into the distinct personalities and traditions of the disciplines: Literature, Art, Mathematics, and Science. At this stage, rather than having the parent integrating all knowledge into his or her own personality, it is good to allow the now distinct self of the student to encounter distinct selves of different teachers and different disciplines: art, science, mathematics, languages. Differentiation into teachers is thus an expression of the differentiation of culture and knowledge into complex systems.

The Third Grade

Theme: Human Systems: the development of human society from the hunting and gathering band to the Ice Age settlement or twentieth-century traditional Arunta or Inuit settlements.

Theory: The evolution from the Gebserian "Archaic" structure to the "Magical." The beginnings of the awareness that the Self is situated in a cultural world in which the instruments and technology that have empowered a sense of self are themselves situated in a history. In other words, the child now begins to be aware of time itself as part of the process of its own empowerment and unfoldment in the world. A strong sense of justice and fair play shows the child's articulation of Self and Other in a growing sense of a moral order. The spirit of the will becomes ensouled with intense feeling in a rage for justice and fair play.

Practice: The exploration of the origins of art, symbolic signs, and religion as they developed together in the rise of human settlements in the Ice Age.

Part of the project of growing up has been the stabilization of the child's sense of self in a body. Before this sense becomes destabilized once again in puberty, it will be timely to consider the story of human culture in the context of the evolution of the body. Here one can embed culture in ecology to consider the Forest ecology and the mammalian body of *Ramapithecus,* the savannah and the emergence of upright posture with *Australopithecus,* and the glacial ecology with the new emphasis on the skin with the development of clothing and the use of mammoth hides to cover the huts of Dolni Vestonice. The year can begin with a focus on mammalian evolution, the primate band, bonobo, and chimpanzee social organization, and the physiology of the early and contemporary human body. In the second semester, the emphasis can shift from the individual body to the social group with explorations of Terra Amata, Dolni Vestonice, and Lascaux. The emergence of ceramics, jewelry, and cave painting will also provide the student with occasions to do intensive craft workshops in ceramics, jewelry, and painting in a consideration of how science, art, and religion are all one in this primordially Magical culture. The year can conclude with a study of shamanism and magic and its survivals in our contemporary world. It will be especially important for young girls to see that the very first portrait in the history of the world is the carved mammoth ivory head of the woman of Dolni Vestonice. This mysterious woman with twisted jaw was the only person buried inside the perimeter of the settlement and was found with several of the "exploding ceramic figurines" of the Great Goddess for which Dolni Vestonice is famous. For this shamanic artist, art and technology, ceramics and divination, were one. Was she "the wounded healer," history's first *"sage femme"*?

The Fourth Grade

Theme: Social Systems, from 10,000 to 3500 B.C.E.

Theory: The evolution from the Gebserian "Magical" to the mythical in the rise of agriculture and the growth of agricultural towns such as Çatal Hüyük (6500–3500 B.C.E.) and the megalithic structures of Western Europe, or

Native American settlements such as Mesa Verde or Taos Pueblo, or, if one lives in the Pacific Northwest, Hawaii, or New Zealand, then other cultural examples closer to home.

Practice: The study of ecology, botany, simple chemistry, archaeoastronomy, sculpture, and the growth of shamanism into religion.

One can begin this year with a consideration of Marshall Sahlin's point that hunters and gatherers were the world's first "leisure society," in which the members of the group only needed to work for fifteen hours a week. Strong emphasis should be placed on the case that woman's knowledge of plants, and their classification systems, set down the beginnings of science and medicine. A workshop could be devoted to actual construction of a wattle and daub hut, a sweathouse lodge, or adobe bricks to give the student a feeling for the construction of human settlements. A field trip could be taken to Mesa Verde or the Taos Pueblo—which is similar to Çatal Hüyük—or to Old Oraibi on the Hopi Mesa—in order to give the student a feeling for human settlements that are embedded in the landscape with a strong reverence for nature and the sacred. Since many contemporary environmentalists have critical ideas about the nature of agriculture, one could consider some of the ideas of Gary Snyder and Wes Jackson and their critiques of contemporary agriculture as a way of understanding just how enormous is this subtle and generationally invisible shift from gathering to gardening.

The rise of ceramics, food storage, and metallurgy provides opportunities to develop units in simple chemistry, and arithmetic modes of understanding quantities. (I am assuming that each teacher can read the primary materials and prepare readers and workbooks so that reading materials can be provided at a fourth-grade level.) The wall paintings and sculptures of Çatal Hüyük provide a wonderful opportunity to study the cultural evolution of painting from cave to wall painting to pottery decoration, the social evolution of the part-time shaman into the full-time priest, the nature and power of ritual and sacrifice, and the nature of sculpture as a form of communication and story-telling.

The rise of the agricultural villages of Old Europe provides an opportunity to study what Marija Gimbutas called "the Civilization of the Goddess." The iconography of the Great Goddess is found from Anatolia through the Balkans, and on throughout the megalithic cultures of Western Europe, from Malta to Avebury and Silbury Hill in England to Newgrange in Ireland. These megalithic structures begin to show evidence of a cosmology of sun and moon and a ritual marking of the four quarters of the year. Even before there were cities and writings on clay tablets, humanity had found a way to store knowledge and pass it on from generation to generation. What Gimbutas calls "the sacred script" of the Old Europe of 5300 to 4300 B.C.E. shows humanity at a high level of development even before the rise of cities in Mesopotamia.

The Fifth Grade

Theme: The rise of the Riverine civilizations: the shift from matristic societies to patriarchal civilizations (3500–1450 B.C.E.)

Theory: The evolution from shamanism to religion, from matristic sacrifice to patriarchal warrior culture, from the immanental and generative Arithmetic Mentality to the transcendental and abstract Geometrical Mentality.

Practice: The study of geometry, irrigation systems, architecture, the simple physics of civil engineering, and the origins of literature in mythology and folklore.

In the third grade, we introduced the nature of simple human systems in the hominid band and the Paleolithic glacial settlement. In the fourth grade we developed this focus into a consideration of the emergence of Megalithic villages and Neolithic towns. Now we come to the full-blown complexity of civilizations, their light and shadow in religion and institutionalized warfare. Our study of civilization, however, should not be restricted to ancient Sumer or Egypt. It should be concerned with the phenomenon of civilization, and a simple way to understand this in a global perspective is to regard all civilizations as being organized hierarchically around military and religious specialists—warriors and priests—and organized around the articulation of a world-space through a new Geometrical Mentality externalized in monumental architecture.

We can also come at this phenomenon in terms of cultural-ecologies by considering these formations as Riverine cultural-ecologies and look at the Nile, the Tigris and Euphrates, the Indus, the Yellow River, and the Usumacinta (the Olmec culture in Mesoamerica) as isomorphic structures of the single cultural phenomenology we wish to identify as "civilization."

We can begin the story of civilization with the story of how Inanna transferred the arts of civilization from Eridu to Erech. Diane Wolkstein's paperback *Inanna: Queen of Heaven and Earth* (New York: Harper & Row, 1983) can be used as a textbook for the teacher, but the parent will have to decide how much of this erotic literature they will want to use this year. Since this poem is about the magic of the list, the mysteries of accumulation, and the numinosity of the storehouse, I would suggest that the tutor in mathematics develop lesson plans in arithmetic that interlock with this Sumerian material.

The rise of monumental architecture in the elevation of the ziggurat provides an opportunity to study city planning and the shift from the communalism of Çatal Hüyük to the class stratification and monumentality of Sumer. Tatiana Proskuriakov has done wonderful drawings of the growth of Mayan pyramids from simple stages for rituals open to all to elaborate ceremonial complexes that were elevated and accessible only to a class of priestly specialists. Gone is the communalism of the village, replaced by the class stratification of the city. Here one can adopt a cross-cultural approach, comparing Mesopotamia and Mesoamerica, ancient Egypt, Mohenjo Daro, and An Yang.[9]

Just as "the tutor of mathematics" is teaching Arithmetic in the context of its historical development in Sumer, I would suggest that "the tutor of writing and poetry" teach the students how to write analyses of poems or papers by asking them to write about Inanna or Enheduanna, the world's first poetess. "The tutor of science" can prepare a course on astronomy and the solar system by linking the discussion to the role of the planets, Mercury and Jupiter, in the poem "Inanna's Descent into the Nether World." Since there is now a burgeoning literature on archaeoastronomy,[10] the linkage of the study of astronomy with archaeology gives the students a chance to visit ancient sites that are oriented to heavenly bodies. At this era of the formation of civilization, the prehistoric power of the Goddess still lingers, and it is Inanna who descends into the Netherworld. The poem is clearly a ritual chant and in contemporary performance can still resonate in our imagination. In later ages, when priestcraft, patriarchy, and writing have consolidated their hold on culture, the descent into the netherworld will be appropriated and transferred to male figures Orpheus, Jesus, and Quetzalcoatl.

By using selections from Diane Wolkstein's little book on Inanna, we have an entire curriculum in microcosm: arithmetic, astronomy, architecture and city planning, mythology, folklore, and the origins of poetry. Since the world's first known poet was a woman, it seems appropriate to our era that the teacher spend some time on Enheduanna and her ode, "The Exaltation of Inanna."[11] If sufficient emphasis had been placed on the alchemical shaman of Dolni Vestonice in the third grade, then by the time we come to Inanna and Enheduanna, young girls should begin to be getting the idea that women are creators of culture: ceramics, botany, agriculture, medicine and midwifery, and astronomy.

If there is a special art teacher for this year, I think a wonderful opportunity could be created in asking the student to paint or create cylinder seals and clay tablets. In this way, the single theme of the global emergence of civilization can organize art, writing, mathematics, science, architecture and city planning, mythology and comparative religious studies into one single year-long course.

In these ancient organizations of society, the genius of civilization was captured by a runaway system of conquest and perpetual warfare, and women were displaced from authority and power in a hierarchical militaristic patriarchy. Recently Leonard Shlain has argued convincingly that this displacement of women is related to the shift from oral culture to writing and the impact this reorganization of hand and eye had on the hemispheric lateralization of the brain.[12] If we want to create a more benign planetary civilization for the future, then we had better understand what went wrong in the very first structural formation of civilization itself. An essential text for the year can be the Babylonian creation epic *Enuma Elish*, but once again we should take a cross-cultural approach in considering the patriarchal domination of women in the Indian *Rig Veda* and the Chinese *Book of Odes*. The "demonization of the Other," whether of savages or women, is a pattern that is mythically expressed in the *Enuma Elish*, in which the ancient Mother Goddess is turned into a monster to be destroyed by the charismatic military hero.

The transition from matristic societies to patriarchal civilizations can also be studied in a comparison of the myth of Isis and Osiris and the *Gilgamesh Epic*. The myth of Isis and Osiris in ancient Egypt presents us with the transition from the mother and mother's brother of matriarchy to the father and the dynastic son of patriarchy. The *Gilgamesh Epic* dramatizes the rise of the heroic male who wishes to challenge the goddess of life and escape the power of death.[13] From conflict we pass on to outright war as we move from the Sumerian myths of Inanna/Ishtar to the *Enuma Elish*, in which Marduk slays the female god Tiamat and builds the city of Babylon out of her dead body. The living *Mater* becomes inert matter. The rise of the military hero, the displacement of the ancient matristic civilization, the enslavement of a serving class—all are chronicled in this document. The *Enuma Elish* also expresses the shift from the ancient Arithmetic Mentality, with the numinosity of the list, to the new Geometrical Mentality, in which the form of the city is the new container that seeks to keep out the female power of death and disintegration. Thus we have a root concept in which the male is archetypally identified with time and form, but the female is associated with chaos, old night, and the disintegrating force of entropy. Before there was math and thermodynamics, there was myth.

The relationship between myth and math is not a simple one of movement from darkness to light, from superstition to scientific law, for myth remains a form of macro-thinking that persists whenever we ask the big questions, "What are we? Where do we come from? Where are we going?" In fact, cultures never outgrow their need for myth, so, to appreciate the relationship between myth and math, mathematics should be taught in its historical context of emergence. As George G. Joseph sees the origins of early algebra in ancient Babylon,[14] the material of this year will provide the teacher of mathematics with the background to introduce the students to ancient Egyptian and Babylonian geometry and the first efforts to develop number theory into algebra. Classes in ceramics could also develop workshops in metallurgy and jewelry making, in which decorative objects develop from copper to bronze, from religious objects and jewelry to the forging of weapons.

In the context of studying the shift from matristic to patriarchal societies, it would be good to focus on Minoan civilization as the twilight of the Goddess, to look back at this culture of high art, architecture, prosperity, and seafaring trade that ended in earthquake, volcanic explosion, and the Mycenaean invasions of patriarchal warriors. Centuries later Sappho would look lovingly back on the legends and reconjure images of this time:

While the full moon rose, young women took their place
around the altar.

In old days Kretan women danced
supply around an altar of love,
crushing the soft flowering grass.[15]

The Sixth Grade

Theme: Prophecy and cultural transformation (1450–350 B.C.E.)

Theory: The role of the individual in the confrontation of evil and suffering and the idealistic transformation of society.

Practice: The study of philosophy, sacred language, and sacred geometry; the masculinist idea of higher mathematics as a vehicle of the soul's transcendence, contrasted to the Eleusinian Mysteries of the immanental Earth Goddess and her daughter.

The fifth grade was concerned with the origins of the ancient civilizations, with the emergence of a social structure in which power is held by warriors and priests. The convivial intimacy of the village is gone, replaced by a new hierarchical organization in which there are top and bottom, literate and illiterate, rich and poor. As the mysteries of religion become less concerned with the reproductive power of the female body and more centered around the secret script the stars write in the sky, religion becomes more elevated and remote, and more under the control of male priests who hold a monopoly on magic through the thaumaturgical power of complex rituals.

The fifth grade was a heavy dose of the reality of a system of militaristic violence that was not merely individual, but societal and systemic. The sixth grade offers the antidote to that environmental poison: the power of the individual to confront the social evil of militaristic violence and articulate a vision of a higher moral order and spiritual way of life.

In fifth grade we ended with the fall of Minoan civilization with volcanic explosion, earthquakes, tidal waves, and clouds of ash darkening the sky. Suddenly people are on the move: the Mycenaeans, the Sea Peoples, the Hebrews. In this time of chaos and confusion, new leaders are needed and are called forth. I suggest we begin our study of this dark time of movement and conquest with parallel examinations of the Hebrew Exodus from Egypt and invasion of Palestine and the Trojan War. Here we can consider two archetypal figures in the articulation of a higher moral worldview, the prophet and the bard, represented by Moses and Homer.

For the continuity of good storytelling, I suggest one reflect back on Minoan civilization at the time of its catastrophic collapse, and then move to the Mycenaeans and the Trojan War. The student will need to be made aware that the Trojan War occurred centuries before Homer's time, but that as myth and legend it allows us to see a culture favored by the ancient Near Eastern goddess of love being overwhelmed by a warrior society favored by the new daughter of the patriarchy, helmeted Athena.

The student in this sixth grade need not be expected to read all of Homer's *Iliad,* but he or she should at least consider one passage in book 22, which expresses the conflict between human compassion and warrior violence. In this episode Priam secretly comes in the night to the tent of Achilles to ask for the return of the body of his son Hector for burial. This dramatic scene captures in miniature the moral issues we will be considering throughout the year's study of the Axial Period.

From Homer and the Homeridae we can pass over to the Old Testament to study Exodus and the migration of the Hebrews from Egypt to Palestine. In our year-long attention to prophecy and cultural transformation, we can study the different forms of prophetic leadership from Moses to Samuel to the kings David and Solomon. I would especially recommend the story of Samson and Delilah in Judges, for the Philistine Sea Peoples may have been bilingual Minoan-Greek-speaking Cypriots involved in a post-Minoan diaspora after the earthquakes and volcanic explosion of Thera. The power of the *femme fatale* over Samson also gives us another occasion to perceive the conflict between the Goddess-worshipping cultures of the Near East and the patriarchal religion of the invading Semitic warriors.[16]

One can also study the transformation of a culture's perception of God through time, from the warrior's deity that helps Samson to go berserk and slay the Philistines to the more refined vision of a universal religion of Second Isaiah, in which all are welcomed into the space of the sacred city of Jerusalem. For the shepherd-prophet Amos, all cities were fallen and corrupt; they embodied the evil and more civilized way of life of the indigenous Canaanites. And, indeed, it was a Canaanite architect, Hiram, who built the great temple for King Solomon.

Even for the atheist, the Old Testament is a wonderful document concerned with revolutionary politics and its problems, with the Weberian routinization of charisma. The people murmur against Moses and prophecy begins to generate a new bureaucracy in the Aaronitic priesthood. The loose amphictyony of tribes cannot hold itself together under a prophetic leader like Samuel and so the people cry out for a military hero, a king, but as kingship grows, so grows the bureaucracy and contradictions of the state. Now the nomads are no longer a simple people worshipping God in a tent, for now King Solomon would have them look toward his temple and the palace when they would pray. King and High Priest once again come between "man" and "his" God. An official bible is created as folk tales and legends and midrash become taken over by priests and scribes working to legitimize the central authority with a new canonical text. Although the Hebrew slaves struggled to break free of the Egyptian Pharaoh, the free Hebrew people do not heed the warning of Samuel and in their own cultural evolution from tribal authority to monarchical institutions, they find themselves in the ironic predicament in which their own legendary King Solomon becomes another kind of Pharaoh.

The legends of King Solomon and his trade with the land of Kush give us an occasion to visit Africa and to examine Kush, ancient Ethiopia, Meroe, and the Nubian expansion into Egypt.[17] From the Sudan we can widen our focus to take in the culture of the Nok in Nigeria, from their earliest development to their innovative iron-working technologies.

From West Africa, we can return to Egypt to consider the conquest of Egypt by the Persian Cambyses II in 525 B.C.E. Legend has it that Pythagoras was studying the ancient mysteries in the temples of Egypt when the land was overrun by the Persian armies and he was taken back to Persia as a prisoner of war. In Persia he was said to have met with the magus Zoroaster and consulted with the Chaldean astrologers. Students can take an imaginative journey with this legendary figure to consider this time of military violence and prophetic vision. We can pass from Pythagoras to Zoroaster to Buddha and Lao Tzu and Confucius in China, and as we examine these prophetic figures we can study the chaotic times in which they lived, trying to articulate a new moral order.[18] This Axial Period is a time of incredible violence in which civilization has crystallized into terror and conquest in the Near East and come apart in post-Zhou chaos in China, but it is also the unbelievable time of Pythagoras; Second Isaiah in Israel; Zoroaster in Persia; Buddha, Kapila, and the author of the *Bhagavad Gita* in India; and Lao Tzu and Confucius in China.

Civilization is a hierarchical structure based on warriorship and priestcraft, so a good place to begin to study the foundations for the Axial Period is in the shift from warrior to philosopher, from priest to sage, beginning with the *Mundaka Upanishad*'s rejection of ritual in favor of contemplation.[19] *The Upanishads* and the Samkhya psychologists present the context for Prince Gautama, who leaves the palace of his father and through the practice of yogic meditation becomes the Enlightened One, the Buddha. So our next reading will be the *Dhammapada.*[20] From India we shall then move to China to consider Lao Tzu's efforts to revitalize the way of the universal feminine.[21] The differing paths of the hermit and the philosopher in the court of the emperor will be considered in contrasting Lao Tzu and Confucius.[22]

From China we can pass over the sea to study the rise of the Chavin, Gallinazo, Salinar, and Nazca cultures in ancient Peru. An examination of South American mythology and the figure of the culture hero Viracocha can provide an occasion for a comparative approach to the study of the mythical figure in the transformation of society and the establishment of civilization and a new moral order. Are Mexico's Quetzalcoatl and South America's Viracocha the same prophetic bearded figure garbed

in local dress, or are the differences between the two more sig-
nificant than their similarities? From our study of the bearded
South American culture hero who wanders the world and brings
a more enlightened culture and way of life to the primitive and
benighted, we extend our horizon of post-catastrophe settlements established by prophetic culture heroes by considering
Quetzalcoatl's moral efforts to eliminate human sacrifice. One
can read the myth of Quetzalcoatl's descent into the underworld
and his reestablishment of human settlements while studying
the Olmec ceremonial center of La Venta and the expansion of
similar ceremonial centers to larger cities such as Teotihuacán.
Certainly, the landscape of the Florentine Codex, with its story
of Quetzalcoatl living in a palace and speaking to his people
from "Crying Out Mountain," seems similar to the Palace of
Quetzalcoatl and the giant Pyramid at the ceremonial center of
Teotihuacán.[23]

The presence of the colossal Negroid heads at the Olmec
sites allows us to raise the controversial question of transoceanic
travel, from western Africa by the black race and northern Africa
by the Semitic Phoenicians.[24] From the world travels of the
Phoenicians, we can return to the Near East to pick up the story
of our legendary culture hero, Pythagoras. Pythagoras is one of
those figures, like King Arthur or Quetzalcoatl, who dwell in a
twilight zone where history is blended with legend and myth.
Along with the capture and release of Pythagoras we can consider the Babylonian captivity of the Hebrews, the Edict of Cyrus
the Great in 538 C.E., the prophecies of Second Isaiah and the
transformation of a merely tribal religion into a great universal
religion. With the release of the Jews and their return to Jerusalem, the city becomes reconstructed in imagination. Through
their exile and suffering, the Hebrews now see Jerusalem not as
a fallen city of evil and civilized Canaanite luxury, but as the
"holy city." The tribal peoples have taken another step in their
cultural evolution into an urban civilization.

The release of Pythagoras allows him to return to Magna
Graecia in Italy. History takes a new turn, as he gathers up
all his knowledge of the esoteric schools of Egypt, Persia, and

India to found a new mystery school in Crotona, one that is intended not for initiates only, but for the secular community as a whole. With the study of the mythic figure of Pythagoras, we have an opportunity to study a visionary synthesis of music, mathematics, and mysticism in the consolidation of the Geometrical Mentality in the establishment of his school in Crotona, the forerunner of Plato's Academy and the modern university. The legendary life of Pythagoras provides the perfect occasion to introduce the study of sacred geometry, musical theory and harmonics, the various modes such as the Dorian and Lydian, the monochord and the system of ratios and proportions, as well as the study of sacred language and cosmology.

A higher feature of civilization is the emergence of the idea of the sacred book and the sacred language. Sumerian became for the Semitic Babylonians what Greek or Latin is for us. In the Jewish and Catholic traditions, at puberty, one begins to study an ancient language as the carrier of one's sacred tradition. One prepares for bar mitzvah or confirmation or becomes an altar boy to memorize the entire Catholic mass in Latin. At this point in the curriculum, a student could elect to begin a study of an ancient sacred language as the carrier of a *cosmology* rather than simply of a *sociology*. The student could elect to begin to work with a tutor in the study of classical Greek, Latin, Hebrew, Sanskrit, or classical Chinese. This form of study of a foreign language is not meant simply for the social game of tourism and ordering food in foreign restaurants, but for passing into the higher mysteries; it constitutes a form of spiritual initiation.

After considering Pythagoras, one can pass into the more traditionally focused study of classical Greek civilization—Greek architecture and sculpture, the origins of Greek theater and the origins of philosophical thought with the Presocratics and Plato. Antigone's moral resistance to Creon can be compared to Demeter's resistance to Zeus and Hades. Woman is basically saying that the moral order of immanental relationship, of mother to daughter or sister to brother is more important than the so-called "higher" and abstract demands of the patriarchal state. With the study of Greek theater, the curriculum introduces a thread on theater and social development that will be picked up again and again in subsequent years.

Another thread is the study of communications media and their impact on the political organization of society. In the fifth grade, we studied the impact of writing in breaking up society into the literate and illiterate; in the sixth grade, we study how the new representation of oral language through the use of the Phoenician alphabet prefigures the emergence of representational government in which elected representatives stand in for the totality of the *polis*.[25]

As an additional narrative transition to link back to the fifth grade, we can consider the Homeric "Hymn to Demeter" and the founding of the Eleusinian Mysteries. This poem of descent into hell can be linked to the fifth grade's study of Inanna's descent into the netherworld. The anger of the Greek Goddess at the patriarchal arrangements of Zeus and Hades can be seen as a return to the ancient values of the civilization of the Goddess of Old Europe. The founding of the temple to the Goddess, with its sacred rituals of initiation, can be read as a new attempt of cultural "retrieval," an effort to re-achieve a village moral order before the rise of warrior culture with its visions of force and mystification of heroic death that we see expressed in the *Iliad*.

The year can close with the contrast between the Immanental Feminine (the ancient Arithmetic Mentality) and the Transcendental Masculine (the new classical Geometric Mentality), with a brief look at Aeschylus's *Oresteia* and Plato's dismissal of the feminine in the *Timaeus*. Here he claims that if one achieves enlightenment, one returns as a male soul to his native star; if one fails, one falls to Earth and is reborn as a woman.[26] The development from ancient to classical civilizations, from Riverine to Transcontinental, can thus be seen as a development of a new mentality. Greek literature and mathematics both articulate the shift from the immanental and generative values of the Arithmetic Mentality of the ancient Great Goddess to the abstract and masculine values of the new transcendental and idealized Geometrical Mentality.

The Seventh Grade

Theme: Universalizing empires and universal religions (350 B.C.E. to 900 C.E.).

Theory: The shift from individual prophetic visions to universal religions and world empires intellectually supported by philosophical visions of a transcultural moral order and how this facilitates the conceptualization of a transcendental abstract code in the emergence of the Algebraic Mentality.

Practice: A study of empires around the world and of the manner in which the institution of the imperial school of philosophy and religion serves to both sanctify and sublimate military violence into a civilized moral order. An examination of the waves of conquest in Hellenistic, Indian, Chinese, Roman, Byzantine, Mesoamerican, Islamic, and Carolingian empires and the schools of religion, philosophy, art, mathematics, and sciences associated with them.

A curriculum is basically a narrative device, a form of storytelling to the young. In order for the curriculum not to degenerate into a heap of disconnected facts and a list of dates, it is important that the parent keep in mind the general thematic structure that relates one year to another. In the fifth grade, we studied the systemic shift to a society of priests and warriors. But the climax of ancient civilizations led to a period of crisis and collapse, brought about by the interlocking agencies of militarism and environmental catastrophe. Out of this dark age, new prophetic figures emerged who tried to re-envision the moral basis of human culture. In the sixth grade, we studied the power of the prophetic individual to challenge the interlocking system of militarism and priestcraft.

In the seventh grade, we study the transformation of the individual prophetic vision into a universal religion and a universalizing empire that seeks to base its legitimacy, not on pure brute force and terror, but on a philosophy of a moral order in which the empire is situated. The institution that is brought forth to meet this need is the imperial school. From Plato's Academy in Athens, the Hellenistic academies in Pergamum and Alexandria, Jundishapur in pre-Islamic Persia, the Buddhist universities of Nalanda and Naropa, the court of the Byzantine Emperor Justinian, the court of Harun al-Rashid in Islamic Baghdad, and the emergence of the Algebraic Mentality with Al-Khawarismi to the articulation of a canon of Confucian classics for an administrative system in the Sui and Tang dynasties in China, and the school of Alcuin in the Carolingian Holy Roman empire, the imperial school becomes the new instrument of cultural governance. Thus the year can begin with Alexander and Aristotle and end with Charlemagne and Alcuin.

In the same era that the emperors are trying to consolidate the reunification in China in the Tang Dynasty, Harun al-Rashid is presiding over one of the most brilliant moments in the civilization of Islam and Charlemagne is trying to bring the Dark Ages to a close and form a new Holy Roman Empire. To further his cultural aims, Charlemagne calls upon Alcuin and the monks of the Celtic monasteries to establish an imperial school that will serve to stabilize civilization in a Christian vision of the moral order. In both the Celtic and Islamic cultures, the emergence of this new transcendental mentality is expressed in the numinosity of the sacred script of calligraphy. In the cultural evolution of consciousness, philosophy and theology have now become part of the intellectual architecture of civilization. Violence is no longer its own sanctification; the sanctification of violence now requires sanctity. As tragic and violent as human history still is, this move represents a major step forward in the development of human culture.

The seventh grade is the period to study the climax and crisis of the classical civilizations, and like the crisis of ancient civilizations, it too is followed, at least in Western Europe and Mesoamerica, by a dark age. Out of this second dark age, the new high medieval civilizations will form and develop, but that is the subject of the eighth grade.

There is a world to cover in this year, and for the teacher and student to keep it all in mind they will need to hold to the structure that I have suggested, which, like a magnetic field, can draw the iron filings of the million facts into a discernible pattern of recognition.

So what I am proposing is not a rapid "mentioning" approach, in which the parent or teacher talks on, mentioning everything that happened everywhere from 350 B.C.E. to 900 C.E., but a comparative, structural approach. Philosophy, religion, art, and architecture are all being rearticulated in a Geometrical Mentality that brings us to the threshold of the Algebraic Mentality in this new cultural phenomenology of empire. This process of rearticulation, and not an avalanche of facts and events, is the real subject matter of the year.

The year should begin with Aristotle and Alexander and track the expansion of Alexandrian culture into India. The combination of Greek sensate humanism and Buddhist sensory transcendence can be studied in the development of Gandharan sculpture. The evolution of consciousness up to a new stage can be considered in the Indian development of algebra as an abstract theory of number, and the development of linguistics in Panini's Sanskrit grammar as a theory of language. As algebra and linguistics take humanity up into an abstract vision of mental process, empire is moving humanity up from the concreteness of tribe and town into a universal vision of transcultural civilization. Alexander's vision of empire can be contrasted to Asoka's efforts in India to extend Buddhism into a politics of enlightened governance. This period of the classical florescence of the Mauryan Empire and Indian civilization in general should be recognized in a major and extensive unit on the civilization of the Indian subcontinent, from the Mauryan era to the time of Harsha Vardhana (605–647 C.E.), who fights back the Huns and contributes to the great Buddhist university, Nalanda.

The expansion of Buddhism from India into China via the Silk Road can provide an occasion to reflect back on the development of China from Han to Tang dynasties, and how cultures

borrow from one another while preserving a cultural unique-
ness of expression.[27] How Buddhism spreads and develops from
India to Southeast Asia to China and Korea provides us with
a chance to appreciate nested forms of culture. What is a "culture," a "civilization," and a "universal religion" that extends
from Sri Lanka to Korea and Japan?

To appreciate the complex dynamic of cultural change, it will
also be important to study the opposed force of cultural exchange; not that of compassion, education, and enlightenment,
but of waves of conquest and destruction. Most atlases of world
history are basically maps of conquest and invasion with roll
calls of military heroes and historical villains.

From our study of Han to Tang dynasties in China, we can
pass once again across the sea to Mesoamerica to revisit our
consideration of the evolution of the prophetic figure Quetzalcoatl and his efforts to eliminate human sacrifice. This unit
should focus on an examination of the spread of the religion
and iconography of the Plumed Serpent from Teotihuacán to
the Toltec-Mayan civilizations in Yucatan and Central America,
where, ironically, human sacrifice is still clearly institutionalized. The temple of the Plumed Serpent at Chichén Itzá clearly
uses the icon of Kulkukan to decorate rather than eliminate
human sacrifice. The presence of jade and the iconography of
the dragon and plumed serpent can provide students an opportunity to understand debate and controversy in historical
scholarship in a consideration of the problem of transoceanic
contacts. Did the ancient Chinese come to Mexico? Did Japanese traders carrying Jomon pottery land on coastal Ecuador?
Did African and Phoenician traders come to the New World?
Are the Phoenicians the bearded figures with aquiline noses we
can see carved into the monuments at Xochicalco? How do
we decide what qualifies as history? How do history, myth,
legend, science fact, and science fiction differ and affect one
another?

After studying the more rooted civilizations of India, China,
and the Americas, it will be appropriate to shift our attention to the nomadic peoples of northern Mexico and the vast

Eurasian continent. Since the settled peoples of both the Old and New Worlds were threatened by invasions from nomadic peoples—Huns and Chichimecs—the dynamic of an imperial civilization is a "periodic attractor" that oscillates between "civilization" (stabile) and "savagery" (labile). From the invasions of the Chichimecs and the fall of Teotihuacán in Mesoamerica, we can return to China to consider the invasions of the Huns and "the crisis of classical civilizations."

To appreciate the unity of the vast land bridge that is Eurasia, we can focus on the impact of the Huns from China to India to Persia and Europe. As we move west from China to Europe, we can stop to consider the indigenous peoples the Huns are displacing, from Persians to Slavs to Ostrogoths to Celts. Since the area and culture of the Celts was once as vast as the Roman hegemony, and since there is a richness of artifacts to consider, we can flash back in time from the fifth century C.E. to the earlier Celtic settlements, from Halstad to the La Tène cultures. And as Celt and Roman compete for dominance in Western Europe, we will need once again to flash back, retracing the formation and development of the civilization of Rome from its beginnings to its end—where we left it as the Huns were about to invade the Roman Empire. For children raised on television and movies, using flashbacks as a device will not be confusing, but it will be important to make certain that the student does realize when he or she is taking a step back in time to consider the formation and development of the culture they are encountering.

At this point our curriculum includes some of the greatest stories of history, those of Julius Caesar, Cleopatra, Augustus, Jesus and the spread of Christianity, and Mohammed and the astonishingly swift spread of Islam. The teacher will need the ability of an Ariosto in his *Orlando Furioso* to keep the *entrelacement* of the plot lines together.

From the breakup of the Roman Empire, the rise of Christianity, and the barbarian invasions, one can move to consider the rise of the Byzantine Empire and its conflict and cultural competition with the Persians. Our study of the imperial school can consider pre-Islamic Jundishapur and post-Islamic Bagh-dad. As the Persian Empire is overwhelmed by the armies of the Prophet Mohammed, we can flashback to tell the story of the rise of Islam, following its spread across Northern Africa to its containment by Charles Martel and Charlemagne.

Traditionally, education was a means of enforcing identity in a symbolic system of self and other, "us" and "them." So French children would read *The Song of Roland* to celebrate the formation of European civilization under Charlemagne, the development of the French language and literary traditions in the *chansons de geste,* and the bravery and manly valor in which the Christian warrior died fighting the evil Islamic Saracens. Patri-otism was the very foundation of education, and it was put in place to ensure that a new generation would be inspired to die in defense of *la patrie.* And, of course, *la patrie,* though a feminine noun, was a patriarchal concept, for girls were meant to stand to the side of power and knit sweaters and socks for the soldiers marching off to war. Even to this day the historical textbooks given to children in France, Japan, or the U.S.A. bear grievous sins of omission and sins of outright fabulation. But our twen-tieth century of world wars has drawn to its close, and today in multicultural Paris or Brooklyn, it is hard to celebrate the old system of Christian versus Muslim.

But precisely in order to affirm our new perspective in time, by contrasting it with the old, it would be good to end the year with Charlemagne and *The Song of Roland* to explore the tra-ditional notion of barriers of conscious identity. In the eighth grade we will go on to show just how permeable a membrane these barriers really are—to see how Islamic science, mathe-matics, music, poetry, and Neoplatonic philosophy influenced European science, philosophy, mathematics, music, poetry, and architecture.

To be sensitive to the complex dynamic of cultural exchange in which a conscious barrier raises the energy of exchange in much the same way that a bridge punctuates the space of the river it crosses, it will be necessary for the teacher to rise to a satellite view of the whole Mediterranean cultural-ecology. One should see the Arabic culture spreading across North Africa, but also reaching down into West Africa.

The Song of Roland will link the closing of the seventh with the beginning of the eighth grade. Although this poem is Christian, it still echoes with many pagan animistic elements: Durendal, the sword of Roland, is itself a character and an ensouled entity which experiences its own apotheosis at the end. From the poem's celebration of the warrior's valor and fealty to his lord, we can pass on to a study of feudalism and the manorial system, as well as to a study of the institution of monasticism. The Plan of St. Gall shows us the workings of a Carolingian monastery and shows us that the monastery was not an ivory tower escape from the real world, but rather a public service corporation that was preserving knowledge, improving agriculture and nutrition, and raising the crafts to higher levels. Indeed, the monasteries will serve later in the establishment of a new institution, the university, begun with the founding of the universities of Bologna in 1100 and Paris in 1150, as well as in the rise of the cathedral movement.

Rather than merely studying the waves of conquest from Alexander the Great to Attila the Hun to the Caliphs of the Prophet, our seventh grade approaches this period as a dialectical pulse of military expansion into new space and philosophical consolidation into form. After the chaos of the fifth century and "the crisis of the classical civilizations," there is an effort to regroup and recivilize. There is the Sui and Tang consolidation of China, the renaissance of Persia under Islam, and the monastic movement to preserve knowledge and civilization in Ireland and Western Europe. From this perspective, it is necessary to shift from the conventional "area studies" approach in which we simply concentrate on China, Persia, or Western Europe to adopt a conceptual approach in which we study these three parallel attempts to rekindle civilization after a dark age. By ending the year with a parallel study of Tang China, the court of Harun al-Rashid and the imperial school of the Irish monk Alcuin under Charlemagne, we can begin to think globally, all the better to act globally and locally today.

The Eighth Grade

Theme: Life and society as a religious work of art: the climax of hierarchical civilizations (900–1416 C.E.).

Theory: The inseparable unity of art, religion, and social structure, in hierarchical civilizations, in which architecture becomes the supreme externalization of human existence into temporal form. From the cathedrals of Europe to the mosques of Isfahan, the Forbidden City of Beijing to the Precolumbian ceremonial centers of the Americas, the ceremonial vision is one of consummate form in which the act of living itself, from drinking tea to riding to the hunt, becomes a work of art. In this entrancement with a transcendental perfection, the Algebraic Mentality is developed and begins to interact with mystical schools such as Sufism, Jewish Kabbalah, and Christian mysticism in the schools of Chartres and Majorca.

Practice: Through an emphasis on art and architecture, we will look at hierarchical civilizations all around the world.

For my generation, "Western Civilization" was a narrative in which all the other cultures of the world were considered uncivilized, so it will be helpful to bear in mind just how primitive European civilization was in 900 when compared to Islamic, West African, Indian, Chinese, or Mayan civilizations. We open the year with King Alfred the Great, who dies in 899, and look at the Anglo-Saxon Chronicle, and with a close reading of *Beowulf*. In studying the movements of peoples, Irish, Anglo-Saxon, and Viking, across Western Europe, we can study the development of feudalism, with its system of loyalties and protection within the fortified castle.

In our study of monasticism, we can consider the conflict between monks and Vikings as almost a centripetal and centrifugal force that is at work in the emergence of European civilization, not unlike the conflict between the Chichimecs and the ceremonial center of Teotihuacán we considered before. Both the Irish monks and the Vikings are the first projections outward to the New World from the classical Mediterranean civilization. The legendary voyages of Brendan, Madoc, and Leif Erikson are the first wave of projection into the Atlantic—legends that will lure later generations of explorers, privateers, pirates, and colonizers, until, at length, a new European civilization will be centered around the Atlantic Ocean and not the Mediterranean.

Following up on our study of possible early transatlantic contact between the Old and New Worlds, we can survey the Native American cultures and civilizations before Columbus, the pueblo cultures of the Anasazi, the Cahokia ceremonial center, and the great climactic hierarchical civilizations of the Inca and Aztec. In the sixth and seventh grades, in our study of Teotihuacán and Chichén Itzá, we encountered the religion of the Plumed Serpent, and how Quetzalcoatl tried to eliminate human sacrifice, but in eighth grade we see how for the Aztecs, the whole religion becomes based on militarism, conquest, and the public theater of human sacrifice. At the end of the year, we will see a similar development in the religion of Jesus in the European form of human sacrifice called the Inquisition.

From the New World, we should take the long way back to Europe, through Japan, studying the Heian culture of Japan (552–1185). A reading of one of the chapters from Lady Murasaki's *Tale of Genji* would be instructive in showing how, in a hierarchical civilization, the sacred and the profane, the quotidian and the sublime, are integrated in an idealized condition in which culture itself becomes a work of art. Prince Genji's choice of exquisite paper and brushwork for his amorous letters, his courtly skill in classical Chinese poetry and music, all reveal the refined sensibility in which life is a supreme artifice for those who live at the top of a hierarchical society.

From our study of Japan we can pass over to consider China, from the cultural florescence of the Sung Dynasties and after during the era of the Mongols, from Genghis Khan to Kubla Khan. At this time China is the most brilliant civilization on the planet. As the rather primitive Europeans find their way along the Silk Road to seek trade with China, we too can work our way back, along with Marco Polo, to Europe along this important route. We can move through the realm of the Seljuk Turks and the Holy Land and flash back in time to study the succession of Crusades and the relations over time between Islam and Christendom,[28] as well as between Western Europe and the Byzantine Empire. From the Holy Land, we can return through North Africa, studying the rise and development of Islam and its flourishing in West Africa. In *Sundiata: An Epic of Old Mali,* we see a black African celebration of Islam as well as of the mythic figure of Alexander the Great. We also see a celebration of the figure of the *griot,* the oral storyteller, and can compare his role with that of the bard in the Celtic cultures of Western Europe. Through the gold trade, the high kingdoms of West Africa are linked to Europe, but Africa is in no way a colony. Its medieval kingdoms are the equal of or superior to the kingdoms of Europe, and at this point in our journey through time and space it would be appropriate to study urbanization in Benin and examine the cultures of medieval West Africa as a whole.

From Africa and the gold trade, we can pass over into Spain to consider the mix of the cultures and religions in Iberia, and the manner in which music, mathematics, Neoplatonic philosophy, and poetry are bringing the world to the edge of a renaissance. With the introduction of the Hindu-Arabic numerals, new forms of bookkeeping, and the development of algebra and higher mathematics, the turn of the thirteenth century into the fourteenth is a period of cultural brilliance, and a step forward in the cultural evolution of consciousness. From the cathedral school of Chartres to Ramón Lull's academy for translation on Majorca to the Arabic-inspired songs crusaders such as Guillaume of Poitiers carried back with them to Provence, to the Sufism that sneaks into *King René's Book of Love,*[29] and Dante's *Paradiso,* and the Persian-Islamic angelology that is raised to new heights in the Jewish synthesis of the *Zohar* and medieval Kabbalah, these medieval cultures were locked into the intimate embraces of love and war. No simple narrative celebration of "Western Civilization" can truly describe the wonderful and complex dynamic of cultural exchange that is animating this time of philosophical transformation, in which art and mathematics take a sudden leap forward.

And indeed from the point of view of a cultural history concerned with the evolution of consciousness, the period does express a sudden leap forward.[30] In the angelic scripts of calligraphy, both in Islamic and Celtic illuminated manuscripts, and in algebra, the "celestial intelligences" of mathematics begin to move in the world of humans. This shift from the concrete to the celestial code is expressed not only in algebra and calligraphy, but also in architecture as cathedrals begin to appear all over Europe. In such figures as Maimonides, Ibn Arabi, Ramón Lull, Giotto, and Dante, the cultural-ecology of the Mediterranean basin comes close to glimpsing a higher civilization. It is a culture in which Jewish, Christian, and Islamic philosophies are influencing one another and preparing the warring kingdoms for a higher world civilization. But, sadly, Europe steps back from this illuminated peak of an enlightened planetary culture and falls into an abyss as plague and Inquisition bring about a dark time of suffering and fundamentalist religious persecution.

In each culture that we pass through, from North and South America to Japan, to China, Central Asia, and North Africa, to Europe, we should notice that despite differences on the surface, the structure of each society is isomorphic. All the societies that we examine in the eighth grade are hierarchically organized around the figures of the high priest and the warrior and ritualized in a religious worldview that energizes sacrificial war, crusade, and *jihad*.

To appreciate what is to come in the ninth grade, both the teacher and the student need to appreciate the structural difference between a hierarchical and a commercial or "modern" civilization. A hierarchical (or sometimes known as a medieval) civilization is structured by a Geometrical Mentality in which there is an elitist center and a provincial periphery with fixed classes and an unchanging order to the nature of things. A modern society is one in which there are competing and conflicting centers with a more complex topology that allows the individual to break loose from the social structure and "move" in space and time to form a new story in the creation of his or her own identity. For a medieval mentality, all value rests in the heaven of a changeless Eternity, and motion is seen as a fallen and sinful condition of vulgar trade and hand labor. For a modern society, motion is the new value, whether it is the motion of money in space that generates interest, or the motion of cannonballs that brings down the fixed walls of castles. In a hierarchical civilization, economic value is based on landowning, and the magnetic field of society is organized around the estates of military knights and the palaces of high priests. The palace and the temple, therefore, are the quintessential architectural expressions that celebrate the form of being in time. Until the new commercialism of the Italian Renaissance, all the agriculturally developed societies around the world were "medieval" hierarchical civilizations ruled by knights and high priests. Although Sung Dynasty China introduced trade, print, and a paper currency, Ming Dynasty China retreated from transoceanic world trade and contracted into a traditional Geometrical Mentality, looked down upon foreigners, and saw all values as coming from the past in the rigidly fixed Mandate of Heaven.

Part of the movement of ideas and goods is, of course, the shadow side of the movement of pests and microbes. Rats as well as humans traveled on trading ships, and the rats that migrated to fourteenth-century Europe brought with them the plague of the Black Death.[31] Some scholars claim that the blossoming of the Italian Renaissance was made possible by this scourge, which created a shortage of labor and thus enhanced the worth and value of the individual artisan. Before we end our study of the climax of hierarchical civilizations by moving on to a study of the early Italian Renaissance in Florence, it will be important to consider plagues as the shadow side of the emergence of the new world space and the new patterns of global travel.

Trading cities like Marco Polo's Venice and the Medicis' Florence begin to assert themselves and make the shift from medieval to modern culture. A new merchant class will begin to sponsor its own form of imperial school in the Florentine Academy of Cosimo de' Medici and Marsilio Ficino. With the fall of the Byzantine Empire in 1453 and the closing of the trade routes to the East, scholars of Greek learning, men such as Gemisthos Plethon, will move from Byzantium to Florence to come under the protection and patronage of the Medicis. The Florentine Academy, under commercial sponsorship, as opposed to the imperial schools we saw in the seventh grade, is the signal of the beginning of the end for medieval civilization. It is a conservative look backward to Greece that energizes a radical leap forward to Renaissance humanism—but that is the story of the ninth grade.

The Ninth Grade

Theme: The shift from medievalism to modernism (1416– 1688).

Theory: The archetypal idea for the whole year of the ninth grade is movement. Our focus is on the emergence of a new mathematical-literary mentality that produces a new narrative for the nature of things in which motion generates value. The motion of money through time produces interest; the motion of the blood in circulation from the heart (not the liver) sustains the life of the body; the motion of sailing vessels produces a New World; the motion of the heavenly bodies produces scientific laws; the motion of cannonballs destroys feudal fortifications and produces new strategic power; and the motion of the individual out of his class produces a new identity of self in the formative picaresque story of a movement from rags to riches. All of these epiphanies of movement constitute the cultural shift from medievalism to modernism in the emergence of a new world economy.

Practice: An integrated studies approach in which the scholarly narratives concerned with the Renaissance, the voyages of discovery, and the rise of European science are brought together in an understanding that these separate descriptions are all partial perceptions of a single cultural transformation.

Integrated Studies Project: The art and science of perspective and the close examination of nature.

The cultural transformation in which medieval kingdoms become modern nation-states can be seen to consist of the following cultural movements:

1. The fifteenth-century projection into Africa by Ming China's Xeng Ho and Portugal's Henry the Navigator expresses the beginnings of the transition to a new culture of global exchange and rearticulation of the world-space. (In order to appreciate the scope of the Ming voyages, one should begin the year with a flashback to consider the beginning of the Ming Dynasty, the expulsion of the Mongols, and the reunification of China.)

2. The shift from medieval economic ideas expressed in "tribute" and "usury" to modern dynamic notions in which the movement of money through space and time generates "interest" and increases value.

3. The shift from the Platonic geometrical universe of perfect spheres, in which motion and change are considered fallen and imperfect states, to the Copernican and Keplerian universe in which two centers dynamically pull the circle into the elliptical orbits of the new planetary system. Building on this Copernican Revolution is Galileo's dynamics of motion and falling bodies. And finishing our period is the new articulation of motion in the calculus of infinitesimals with Newton and Leibniz. In dependent co-origination with this new science of motion is the new technology of firearms and artillery, which brings down the armored knight and the walled fortresses of feudalism, and ushers in a new era of capitalistic nation-states.

4. The shift from manuscript to printed book as the dominant form of communication, and the impact this democratization of information has on releasing the individual from his or her dependence on the clergy for the interpretation of his or her place in nature and society.

5. The rise of the individual and his or her separation from traditional systems of authoritarian domination expressed by

feudalism and medieval Catholicism. The solitary self begins to have its own trajectory through space and time, from the Old World to the New, and this movement forms itself into the individual life as a "story." This cultural change is expressed in the shift from the aristocratic epic to the bourgeois novel as the emergent literary form.

6. Coeval with the rise of the novel with its picaresque structure of "rags to riches" is the rise of the individual as scientist, as a hero making his way through the world. Descartes's *Discourse on Method* should be taught as a picaresque narrative, as the story of a soldier of fortune finding his way in the world through trial and error. In its deep structure, the *Discourse on Method* is analogous to *Lazarillo de Tormes,* the sixteenth-century narrative of a little beggar boy who finds his way from poverty to comfort. The genius of Cervantes's rendering of the Spanish picaresque tradition in *Don Quixote* is that he is showing the modern individual pursuing his personal fantasy-reality by (paradoxically) striving to recover the medieval past of knighthood. The medieval content of the mind of the Knight of La Mancha camouflages the modern structure of his consciousness. In fact, madness, whether it is explored in *Hamlet, King Lear,* or *Don Quixote* is one of the major concerns of this time precisely because the individual is now more profoundly alone and set loose into a greatly expanded universe than had been the case for feudal subjects in medieval cultures.

We begin the year with China advancing and becoming the world's leading civilization, then retreating from the projection into a world civilization; and we end the year with Europe articulating the shift from a medieval empire to a modern economy and new philosophy in the new ideas of the philosopher and the philosophical academy in Europe and America. The figure of Leibniz—who as an energetic correspondent with the learned societies of his day was in himself the first World Wide Web—can serve as an archetypal figure, both in his understanding of motion and because of his globalizing efforts to think through the ancient Chinese conception of change in the

I Ching, as expressed in his *Discourse on the Natural Theology of the Chinese.*[32] The year can begin and end with China to ponder the paradox that in spite of being the world's most advanced civilization, Ming China retreated into a medieval Geometric Mentality, and Europe expanded. And so it is that English and not Chinese has become the contemporary language of globalization.

Some Important Ideas for Maintaining the Thematic Unity of the Year

In an artistic structure of *aria da capo,* the year opens with the retreat from global projection by China and ends with Leibniz's effort to "retrieve" the ancient Chinese pre-Geometrical understanding of movement and change expressed in the *I Ching.*

The shift of the capital of China from coastal Nanking to inland Peking represents the contraction of China into a Geometrical Mentality and expresses a lack of imagination necessary to effect the shift into a new mathematical imagination of the world. The Ming Empire crystallized into a Geometrical Mentality in which all value was at the imperial center and all economic relations were to be structured as "tribute" in which the periphery contributed to the imperial center.[33]

Europe moves into the vacuum left by Ming China and, because of its coevolutionary system of feedback between economics and science, it establishes cultural dominance. As a result we live in a European global civilization in which China is only now seeking to correct for its previous lack of imagination; but notice that China continues to assert itself in traditional geometrical and imperial terms, in which the center controls the periphery (Tibet, Hong Kong, and Taiwan) and a monocrop culture distrusts polycentrism and diversity, clinging to a single communist ideology with emotionally embedded notions of racial and cultural superiority.

In other words, to understand our edge of history in the shift from nationalism to globalization, we have to go back to the other edge of history and understand the shift from medieval empires to modernist middle-class nation-states.

This shift from the Geometrical Mentality to the Galilean Dynamical Mentality involves a shift from a geometrical spatialization of the world-picture, in which there is a single imperial center with a single authority seated in Rome or Peking, to a polycentric world economy, in which a globally mobile middle class trades with enemies and infidels through the means of new forms of travel (caravels) and new forms of information (printed books). (Ironically, Ming Chinese ships had been larger, and, of course, the Chinese had invented printing centuries before.) Thus we are studying the rise of a European global civilization through the rise of new systems of banking, world trade, capital formation and investment; a new mathematical imagination; new systems of science, technology, and communication; and new forms of highly untraditional individualization expressed in painting, with its shift from iconic group values to individual perspective and portraiture, new literary genres with the novel, and new theories of knowledge in the shift from theology to an empiricist and secular scientific philosophy. This interacting system of mutually affecting causes generates an emergent domain—not a single empire with a single imperial center, but a polycentric world economy.

Our global emphasis should be maintained by concentrating on China, Latin America, Europe, West Africa, and North America. In the tenth grade, the focus can return to India, but since the rise of a new world economy of baroque wealth and display is supported upon a foundation of slavery,[34] we should examine the modernist transformation of traditional African slavery and focus on the cultural relations, for example, between Brazil and Africa.

Suggested Tie-In with Science

Theme: The transformation of sight and space.

Core Disciplines: Astronomy, physics, and physiology.

The ninth grade should focus on the transformation of sight and space, in which new worlds become part of an expanded conceptual reality. Hitherto invisible spaces like America become part of the world; hitherto invisible forces like gravity, microscopic life, economic interest, and motion become articulated in a new image of the solar system, the planet, the body politic, and the human body in Renaissance art and physiology. Since with the ninth grade we pass over into the traditionally defined stage of "high school," I shall break down the narrative into an outline by months.

September

We should begin the year with the oceanic voyages and the articulation of the world-space. We can start with the voyages of the Chinese Zheng He to India, the Persian Gulf, and Africa from 1405 to 1433. We can focus on how the Chinese came close to creating a modern global civilization, but withdrew because the rulers could not effect the shift to a new mathematical imagination of the world-space. (This shows the student just how important mathematics is to culture and the Real World.)

The early Ming emperors had no desire to return to the multi-state system of the Song; their goal was to reassert Chinese centrality in East Asia on the model of the Han or Tang dynasties. They re-established the tribute system, posited on the moral centrality of the Chinese emperor who received tribute and conferred largesse. Taizu forbade private foreign trade, wanting all exchange to occur through the framework of this tribute system. The third emperor, Chengzu, sent out emissaries to visit potential tributary states. The grandest of these were the overseas voyages of 1405 to 1433, led by one of his most trusted servants, the Muslim eunuch Zheng He. The huge flotilla assembled for the first expedition carried 27,000 men on sixty-two large and 225 small ships, the largest of which was 440 feet long. The first three voyages stopped at places as distant as India. The fourth went further to Hormuz on the Persian Gulf, and the last three as far as the east coast of Africa. Unlike the European oceanic expeditions later in the fifteenth century, trade and exploration were not the primary motive behind these voyages; their purpose instead was to enroll far-flung states into the Ming tributary system. They were abandoned when court officials persuaded later emperors that they were not cost-efficient.[35]

A textbook that may serve for September is the Time Warner *TimeFrame, A.D. 1400–1500: Voyages of Discovery.* After a consideration of China, one can then contrast it with the Italian and Portuguese projections into the new world-space and the different imagination they bring to it, basing their explorations on trade rather than tribute. (In essence, this expresses the shift from medievalism to modernism.) The projection of Portugal south along the coast of West Africa provides an occasion for revisiting these cultures and noticing that there are great cities, such as Benin, flourishing with highly developed art forms. At the opening of the ninth grade, the African cultures are the equal to the European; it is only at the end of our period that the new science of Newton and Leibniz are beginning to take Europe into a new scientific and technological culture that will open up a new bifurcation into which the high kingdoms of Africa and the Ottoman Empire do not seek to move. This bifurcation becomes the split between modernizing and traditionalist cultures, a split that remains as polarizing today as it was then.

October

With a study of Renaissance Florence, we can consider the rise of banking and the leadership of the Medicis, and the shift of the intellectual center from Byzantium to the new Florentine Academy founded by Cosimo de' Medici and directed by Ficino. Through Florence, we can study the Italian Renaissance as a whole. Here I would think a whole "unit" on painting can be developed. For example, the shift from the iconic qualities of Cimabue to the more narrative qualities of Giotto; the rise of perspective in Alberti and Leonardo; the attention to landscape as more than simply a stage for a religious event. This shift of attention, especially evident in Bellini and Brueghel, later becomes a pronounced effort to understand the dynamics of motion in clouds, as in Ruysdael, or the dynamics of motion in crowds, as in Altdorfer's *Battle of Issus*. One could contrast the Zeno-like understanding of motion in the cartoonlike freeze-frames of medieval painting, such as we see in Giovanni di Paola's *St. John Baptizing in the Desert,* with Altdorfer's perspectival *Battle of Issus.* And, of course, great emphasis should be placed on the shift of attention in portraiture from saints to living individuals.

Along with painting, one will, of course, need to consider the transformations in architecture from the Gothic to the Renaissance styles. Once again, an in-depth unit on a single building, such as Brunelleschi's contribution to the cathedral in Florence, may be more effective for the student than a rapid survey.

November

From the study of the rise of world trade and banking in Italy, and the competing and polycentric system of trading cities that have as their phase-space a world-economy (Florence, Genoa, Venice), I would pass over into the Portuguese, Spanish, Dutch, and English oceanic extensions. Here one can contrast the more "primitive" culture of Portugal with the high cultures of the powerful empires of West Africa.

December

The competition between Spain and England will provide us with an opportunity to study the Reformation and the importance of Protestantism in consolidating the growth of trade and middle-class values. The rise of printing (McLuhan's "Gutenberg Galaxy") serves to empower the individual by placing knowledge in his or her own hands. The transformation of education by the printing industry means that knowledge and education are no longer in the hands of the Church but are being advanced by business. England breaks away from the papacy and because of it, the English trading class is free to ignore papal strictures against usury:

During the German discussions in the 1520s of the legitimacy or illegitimacy of the customary practices of commerce, according to the teachings of scripture and the Church, the moderates among the reformers conceded the need for secular commercial use of prohibited machinery such as interest on loans. Luther's close collaborator, Philip Melanchthon, for instance, considered that secular magistrates could allow interest on loans, on the grounds that it was an essential part of business practice and harmed no one. In a public disputation on the topic, he contended that "the law of Christ" was not necessarily to be taken as the basis for the organization of secular society, allowing the magistrates the right to rule in accordance with civil law. Christians, however, did not have to borrow or lend, no matter what the secular ruler allowed.

The thrust of such arguments was to separate spiritual belief from secular business practice, allowing the individual to act in his best commercial interests and leave the matter of Christian morality to be settled elsewhere (in his private religious observance.) ...

The Spanish ambassador in London, Bernardino de Mendoza, watched with growing concern the increasing advantage the English were gaining over the Catholic merchants in the East. In May 1582 he advised Philip II of Spain of the way the English were profiting from their punishment by the Pope....

In January of 1581 he had already warned that the English were not only sending out a "multitude of vessels to Morocco with arms and munitions, but have now begun to trade with the Ottoman Empire, whither they take tin and other prohibited goods to the Turks." Mendoza's concern was well-founded. In spite of their comparatively late arrival on the eastern trading scene, the English merchant companies were now in a position to pursue their trading profit, in an entirely secular commercial context, free from the operating constraints of international religious law.[36]

From the Reformation on the continent, we can pass over to England to consider Henry VIII's break with the Church, the ascent of Elizabeth, and the conflict with Spain. Since Bruno was thought to be a spy for the English within the French embassy, we can consider English history on two tracks. One line is the traditional one concerned with the influence of the Italian Renaissance on the English Renaissance, the rise of modern English in the poetry of Wyatt and Surrey, Spenser, Sydney, and Shakespeare, but the other is "the Rosicrucian Enlightenment" of Frances Yates, in which John Dee and Giordano Bruno are special agents for the Protestant Reformation against the forces of the Spanish Counter-Reformation.[37] The defeat of the Spanish Armada (which, according to Ralph Abraham, came about because of the superior navigational mathematics given to the British navy by John Dee) and the Thirty Years' War should not be looked upon through simple schoolboy narratives of battles and heroic nationalisms, but as a larger cultural struggle in which the Inquisition is seen as part of an effort to destroy secularization and modernization. Shakespeare's *Henry V* could be read here as an expression of English patriotism in the positive afterglow of the defeat of the Spanish Armada.

January

In considering Spain's conflict with England, we go on to consider the Spanish maritime projection in the conquests of Mexico and Peru to dramatize once more the radical difference between modernism and medievalism. As Spain seeks to destroy one Aztec empire, it substitutes its own tributary system and crystallizes into an economic fundamentalism based on the metallic values of holding gold and silver rather than expanding economies through circulation. (Similarly, the gold and silver used to trade with China simply disappears, as the Ming Chinese rulers hoard it, take it out of circulation, and resist expanding into the circulations of a currency-based economy which Sung Dynasty China had introduced in the first place.) Spain also crystallizes into the religious fundamentalism of the Inquisition and seeks to eliminate all diversity. (Students of Spanish here may wish to read *Brevísima relación de la destrucción de las Indias* by Bartolomé de las Casas.)

The conquest of Mexico provides an occasion to appreciate the collision between medieval and modern worldviews and the confrontation between magic and technology, plagues and people. What helps a small band conquer a vast empire is the invisible microbes the invaders carry with them. The smallpox introduced by the Europeans to the New World decimates the native population. Along with this transportation of microbes is a transportation of plants. The tobacco and the potato plants of the New World will eventually have a disastrous impact on European civilization as cancer and the Irish potato famine kill millions. Since the World Health Organization now claims that we are at another one of these thresholds in which the shadow side of global travel is about to generate another Black Death, it may be worth stopping to consider the complete phenomenology of cultural and ecological transmissions.

February

In 1600, Giordano Bruno is burned at the stake by the Inquisition. In Prague in 1618 the Thirty Years' War begins. Descartes is a soldier in this war and is stationed in Bohemia during the winter. One way to construct a "unit" that can capture the larger historical forces at work is to focus on the lives of Descartes and Galileo. One could read merely the opening of Descartes's *Discourse on Method* to see it as a picaresque narrative, the story not of a doctor of the Church, but of a soldier of fortune, bouncing from one incident to another, seeking to discover the truth through trial and error. The second unit could focus on the trial of Galileo in 1633, on the conflict between the old authoritarian, single-centered Geometrical Mentality and the new Dynamical Mentality. In considering Galileo, we can stop to consider the whole shift from the Ptolemaic solar system to Copernicus and Kepler. In the analytic geometry of Descartes, one can study the philosopher's efforts to resolve the conflict between stasis and dynamics by creating a new Cartesian grid for the articulation of motion.

In understanding the fundamentalism of the Inquisition as a rigid literalization of value, in which a structural transformation of mentality is resisted by holding to the old ways, it would be worth considering the contrast between Spain and the Netherlands. Spain expels the Jews in 1492, energizes the Inquisition, and seeks to expand into the New World in a classical fashion by enslaving the Indians and holding on to value in the literal forms of gold and silver. Its economic and religious fundamentalisms lock it into a conservative worldview that blocks its entry into modernism all the way up into the twentieth century until the death of Generalissimo Franco.

The Netherlands, by contrast, is tiny, yet its economic phase-space is vast. Its energizing of the Protestant Reformation and the spirit of capitalism creates a culture of information (capitalistic banking) rather than metal. It becomes so wealthy that the Bank of Amsterdam becomes the model for the founding of the Bank of England in 1688. Throughout the late seventeenth and early eighteenth century, it is the Netherlands that is the source of England's coming greatness, and it is the Netherlands that lends England the money to finance the rebuilding of its infrastructure of canals and roads that paves the way for England's industrial revolution in the later eighteenth century.

The wars of religion of the sixteenth and seventeenth century, whether Montezuma versus Cortés, or Protestant England, the Netherlands, and Bohemia versus Spain and Austria, are not simply national conflicts. They are collisions of worldviews in which decidedly different mentalities are on opposite sides of the battle.

March

It would be unfair to present Spain only as the source of the Inquisition and the destruction of the Indians in Mexico, so it is important for the sense of balance to consider the golden age of Spanish literature to present Spain as the source of the modern novel. One can begin with *Lazarillo de Tormes* (1548) to look at the archetypal pattern of the picaresque narrative that lies behind Descartes's *Discourse on Method* and is the ancestor of

Gil Blas and *Moll Flanders.* Then we can move on to selections from *Don Quixote* (1605, 1615) to consider the crisis of the individual cut loose from faith, and the new psychological condition in which personal fantasy challenges culture in a more complex relationship of imagination and perception, madness and reason.

April

In the shift from feudalism and Christendom, in which Latin is the language of scholarship, to nations in which the merchant classes are competing for world dominance, the national language begins to take on a singular importance in the construction of cultural identity. One should do a "unit" here on the nature of theater and the manner in which the stage becomes a place for the performance of the English language with Shakespeare, the Spanish language with Lope de Vega and Calderón de la Barca, and the French language with Molière and Racine. The changing architecture of the theater also represents a movement away from the aristocratic masque to a more public space in which the classes come together in a celebration of their sense of being English, French, or Spanish. One could flash back to trace the evolution of the politics of performance-spaces to consider the Greek and Roman theater, the medieval mystery plays on the steps of the cathedral or on carts in the public markets. One could also contrast the rural and pagan ritual elements in *commedia dell'arte* with the more aristocratic masques of Inigo Jones. One could expand this architectural study to contrast the forms of theater to that of churches in the Reformation and Counter-Reformation, and consider the tension between public space as sacred and profane in the closing of the theater in Puritan, Cromwellian England, and then the baroque elaboration of theater in the 1660s and '70s with Molière and Racine.

May

The evolution from Renaissance to Baroque can be seen as a reappropriation of middle-class expansion into new space, a retreat back into the consolidations of form in the aristocracy and the new culture of wealth. And it is important to see that the new gaudy display of baroque wealth is founded upon the new global economy of slavery. This industrialization of slavery and turning it into a massive "economy of scale" for the production of sugar and tobacco is quite different from traditional African slavery, so the student should be asked to take a closer look at these two different organizations of domination, African and European.

European national theaters, national literatures, and national science now come under the patronage of monarchy. With the founding of the Royal Society in England, science moves from being a threat to the social order to becoming a prop for the monarchy. The new science is not all mechanical, but has its mystical side as well. We can see mysticism in Boyle's chemistry, which hovers between modernism and alchemy, or in Newton's black box, which contains his magical computations of the prophecies of Daniel and the sacred measures of the temple of Jerusalem.[38] The dreams and visionary experiences of Descartes and Pascal also can serve to show that these bogeymen of the Cartesian paradigm are not as Cartesian as they are often made out to be.

The schizophrenia of this shift from religion to science in what Whitehead called "the Century of Genius" should be pointed out by contrasting the genius with the madness of the Inquisition, the massacre of women in the witch trials, and the genocide of the Thirty Years' War. A consideration of Frances Yates's theories of "the Rosicrucian Enlightenment" and the evolution of the Royal Society can bring us to study the place of science in the new civilization of Western Europe. Newton and Leibniz consummate the era by achieving the philosophical study of motion and gravitational dynamics in the calculus, but Newton also embodies the new relationship of economics and science in that he also served as Chancellor of the Exchequer.

June

I would close the year with a look at Leibniz, his serving as founding president of the scientific academy of Berlin, and the manner in which these new academies and societies are preparing the way for the Enlightenment. This close to the year will help us to link the ninth grade with the tenth, which will consider the caricature of Leibniz in Voltaire's *Candide* and the development of the Age of Reason into the Enlightenment. One should take a transatlantic view and consider the founding of Yale and Harvard and the Philosophical Society in Philadelphia as part of this general cultural movement. In spite of religious wars, witch trials and other persecutions in the Inquisition and global slavery, the age of the wars of religion ends with science firmly in place. The image of the natural philosopher in the personhood of Newton and Leibniz is set on high in baroque apotheosis to replace the hagiography of earlier times. The scientist becomes the avatar of the New Age and will be the inspiration for Franklin and Jefferson.

To round off the year and end as we began, with China, I would suggest we consider Leibniz's efforts to understand the *I Ching* in his book, *Discourse of the Natural Theology of the Chinese*. The book is a little later than our period and takes us into the eighteenth century, but that too can serve as preparation for the tenth grade. Leibniz's effort to "retrieve" the pre-Geometrical articulation of change and transformation in ancient China in the context of Enlightenment Europe is a prophetic step toward a planetary culture.

Also to close on an equally global note, I would consider the impact of perspectival consciousness (see Jean Gebser's discussion of the importance of this structure of consciousness) in China by studying the painting *One Hundred Horses* by Giuseppe Castiglione, a Jesuit in China (1688–1766). One could study the nonperspectival articulation of space in traditional Chinese painting, as well as the wedding of West and East in this fascinating work.

Tenth Grade

Theme: Revolution and the rise of the individual (1688–1851).

Theory: The archetypal idea of grade nine is movement; in grade ten it is time—that intense sense of contemporaneity that impels the idea of revolution. The expansion of European civilization into the New World brings with it a new expansion and empowerment of the middle class. With the democratization of information through printing, the priest and the knight no longer hold the traditional structure of civilization. The scientist, the inventor, and the artist become new charismatic embodiments of a time of change. The dissenting minister with his congregation, the scientist and inventor with their learned societies, the revolutionary with his pamphlets and printing press, and the artist as a charismatic genius with his own following, all create a new cultural myth of individuality that transforms the millennia-old formations of domination and governance.

Practice: The study of the interrelationships between the English Revolution, the Enlightenment, the Industrial Revolution, the American and French Revolutions, and the European Revolutions of 1848 in creating a new global political culture.

Integrated Studies Project: Portraiture and individuation; art and electricity: the case of Frankenstein; the Romantic artist as shaman and prophet: the case of Beethoven.

In the ninth grade, we examined the cultural bifurcation in which European civilization branched off into a new mathematical mentality based on motion in space. In the tenth grade, we examine how this Galilean Dynamical Mentality calls forth new social, economic, and political movements in the Enlightenment and the revolutions in the Americas and Europe. A complex dynamical system of feedbacks of mathematics, technology, and capital formation creates an emergent condition of societal innovation in which Europe enters into a society that is completely different from the Ottoman, West African, and Qing Empires. Although academic historians no longer like to use the term "medieval," I still find the term useful in contrasting two completely different world economies and cultures. Traditional hierarchical societies are based upon the value of land and are organized in fixed classes, but in the Galilean Dynamical Mentality, motion creates a phase-space that becomes the new conceptual domain of the complex dynamical system of a polycentric world economy.

Medieval mentalities store gold and take it out of circulation. (This mentality actually contributed to the contraction of the Ming Empire and the decline of global Chinese influence.) The phase-space of the modern mentality is the global economy, in which the future is created as a cognitive domain through the national debt and the management of currencies of exchange through the founding of a national bank. This new world economy is a phase-space and not simply a geographically located territory; it is based upon the imaginary space of global finance and the imaginal temporality of redemption through the future in bonds and national indebtedness articulated through such radically novel institutions as the Bank of England. As the British Empire dynamically expands into this new cognitive domain, Islamic, Indian, and Chinese civilization decline as they contract or remain fixed within the state-space of a medieval Geometrical Mentality. As this new European industrial civilization expands, the strong West African medieval kingdoms that, unlike their counterparts in Mexico and Peru, had always been able to keep European expansion at bay by controlling their own contributions to the slave trade, begin to cave in under the impact of the European industrial revolution.

Tie-In with a Scientific Curriculum

Theme: The transformation of time.

Core Disciplines: Geology and chemistry.

The tenth grade should focus on the expansion of time, which comes with the founding of geology and the new understanding of the geostrophic cycle in the work of Hutton. This new science involves a paradigm shift from reading the text of the Bible to reading the text of the landscape with its greater eons of geological time. The rise of chemistry, with its appreciation of the new explosive power of simultaneous interactions, should be studied and integrated with the new chemistry of revolutionary explosion and transformation. The rise of the individual as a mythic story of movement and transformation, from rags to riches, from obscurity to world fame, as in the cases of Newton and Leibniz, should be examined as the construction of a new narrative. Society is no longer a medieval and changeless Chain of Being, as in the Chinese "Mandate from Heaven" for the Emperor, but rather a dynamic movement of time. With the founding of European social science with Giambattista Vico, a new historical story of progressive movement in time from forest-dwelling to village agriculture to urban civilization begins to challenge the biblical narrative of the Fall and the Flood.

This tie-in with science thus focuses on the rise of chemistry, geology, and economics in the eighteenth century, and the rise of thermodynamics in the early nineteenth century. This historical period is also witnessing the revolutionary conceptual shift of the idea of sovereignty from the king to the Parliament in England, and to the people in general in the United States and France. Simultaneously, there occurs a shift in the locus of values from the feudal community, with its web of obligations, to the individual citizen. Nature was once a static backdrop to a static society of fixed estates; through the narratives of natural history, it becomes a story of the unfoldment of a new identity through time.

Possible Subjects for Integrated Studies

A unit that could bring performing arts into cultural history would be an in-depth study of Mozart's opera *The Magic Flute*. Since the year's theme is revolution, a look at the role of Freemasonry in the Enlightenment would be interesting, enabling the student to consider Mozart, Washington, and Jefferson as part of a larger cultural movement. The archaic Queen of the Night in *The Magic Flute* is not merely the prehistoric matriarch; she is also an image of a reactionary Holy Mother Church fighting to keep her children out of the clutches of the initiates of the Reformation. Although opera is not generally a favorite art form for teenagers, this particular opera is certainly easier than most to appreciate, and could serve to illuminate other themes, such as the emergence of the modern artist as more than a mere domestic servant of the aristocracy. Here Milos Forman's film *Amadeus* could serve to provide the student with vivid images of aristocratic hubris.

Another unit for bringing performing arts, media studies, and cultural history together is to examine the psychological development of the string quartet by Beethoven. Previously, the string quartet had been chamber music, a musical conversation among friends and light entertainment for amateurs and courtiers in the great houses of the aristocracy. But in the middle quartets, Beethoven expands the art form into virtuoso performances intended for the new space of the public concert hall.[39] Then, in the late quartets, the music becomes more interiorized and mystical (especially in the opening movement of the C sharp Minor, the Fourteenth, and the third movement of the F Major, the Sixteenth). Perhaps because of the interiorization brought about by his own deafness, Beethoven stretches the interface between silence and music, instant and continuum, in an exploration of mood, states of consciousness, and time itself as the architecture of the extensive field of consciousness. It is as if the instruments were no longer voices in a conversation, or virtuosos contesting in a public display of excellence, but the subtle bodies of incarnation and the subpersonalities of individuation itself. In this development, music is prophetic and a century ahead of psychology.

The tie-in with media studies would be to consider the shift from the position of the musician as talented domestic servant to The Artist as prophet and high priest of a newly emergent religion for a newly emergent secular society. Jacques Attali, who was the economic adviser to President Mitterand in France, has put forth the interesting theory that there are four networks in the development of music, and that music prophetically prefigures the economic reconstruction of society. These four networks are: (1) *sacrificial ritual;* (2) *representation;* (3) *repetition;* and (4) *composition.*[40] The network of ritual is expressed in peasants piping in the field; representation is written music in performance, such as Mozart in concert before the Archbishop of Salzburg; repetition is Toscanini in the recording studio; and composition is the composer alone with God, a creative act that takes place out of the exchanges of commerce. Beethoven would be a good choice for our study of "Revolution and the Rise of the Individual" because his overture to Goethe's *Egmont* and his opera *Fidelio* celebrate liberation from tyranny; and his *Eroica* symphony captures the complexity of the relationship between celebration of the individual in the heroic figure of Napoleon, and political apotheosis of the self-inflated figure of the Emperor. Deaf Beethoven himself "retrieves" the archaic figure of the shaman as "wounded healer" and sets down a new archetypal pattern of the solitary and shamanic artist in the industrial world.

If the teacher has an extensive unit on music in the first semester, then I suggest a more architectural unit for the second semester. Our previous unit on cathedrals in the ninth year can here be followed with a unit on the Great Exhibition of 1851 in London. We can focus on London as the world-city of the new global economy, on Paxton's architecture of wrought iron and glass that looks forward to Bauhaus, and the cultural "retrieval" of medievalism as a camouflage for industrialism. The debates in Parliament over what to do with the trees in Hyde Park, and the consequent decision to build the Crystal Palace to enclose them signals that culture is now surrounding nature for the first time in human history. Thus the Crystal Palace anticipates not only Bauhaus, but also Biosphere II in Oracle, Arizona.

Since our theme is individuation, I suggest that the student begin to prepare for college-level writing to come by selecting one individual for an in-depth essay concerned with character and contradiction, revelation and camouflage. Rousseau and Jefferson both reveal and conceal, and both were certainly full of contradictions, but Napoleon or Simón Bolívar, Mozart or Beethoven, George Sand or Mary Shelley are also good examples.

One could also do a unit on urbanization and literature by comparing Dickens's London with Balzac's Paris, or a study of science and painting in the new consciousness of heat by looking at Turner and Carnot.[41]

September—The Democratic Mythos

To tie in with our study of theater and national identity in the ninth grade, and to introduce the student to the idea that the construction of history is an act of the imagination that affects personal identity, I suggest we begin with an artistic work on a historical revolt: Schiller's *Wilhelm Tell.* Although this work is probably more accessible to German and Swiss schoolchildren than to Americans, it raises distinctly American issues concerning arms and the citizen, citizen militias, and our whole NRA–Charlton Heston cult of the armed individual defending himself against the state. In contemporary America, the rural West is very individualistic, anarchic, and violent, and it regards the federal government as the alien empire of a Rockefeller-Trilateral world conspiracy, much as the rural Swiss peasant of Schiller's drama looked upon the Hapsburg Empire as an alien presence.

Beginning the year with the revolt of the Swiss cantons against the Hapsburg Empire is also useful in connecting to the revolts of the Dutch, because the Swiss served as an example to the Dutch of a small and unaristocratic society that was able to rise up and defeat the Hapsburgs and the Burgundians—traditional enemies and conquerors of the Dutch as well. The Swiss cantons were not a state but simply an oath-bound federation for mutual defense—an *Eidgenosenschaft,* which served as a model for the *Bondgenootschap* of the not-so-united United Provinces of the Netherlands. The success of the Dutch helped to inspire the

English, in their turn, to reject the Counter-Reformation forces of the Catholic Stuarts and to establish a new society in which sovereignty was no longer to be defined as the sovereign, but as the Parliament, in which the king, lords, and commons together embodied the new body politic.

Although *Wilhelm Tell* is a dated historical piece, it is precisely dated to the historical period we are studying, so it is worth considering. Schiller was a political refugee who had to flee the domination of the Duke of Baden-Württemburg, a feudal lord who would not allow Schiller to become a playwright but insisted that he serve as a doctor in his army. Schiller expresses the image of the artist as the new man of a new age. Indeed, he was made an honorary citizen of the French Revolution, so he seems an appropriate figure with which to announce our theme of "Revolution and the Rise of the Individual." Statues of both Schiller and Beethoven are in New York's Central Park, so it might be worthwhile understanding why they are there as part of our own American revolutionary spirit.

I would imagine that it would take one week to discuss *Wilhelm Tell*, and two weeks to review the Civil War in England with Cromwell and his "ethnic cleansing" of the Catholics in Drogheda, Ireland, and the Anglo-Dutch rivalry, conflict and cultural interpenetration that leads up to the English Glorious Revolution. The Glorious Revolution itself can be seen as a war of religion, but it does express the consolidation of the spirit of the Reformation in the new space of the sovereignty of the Parliamentary nation-state, with its bifurcation from land to capital as the basis of value and the new ground for economic transactions.

October—The Glorious Revolution and the Founding of the Bank of England

In my high-school days, the bias of Anglo-American narratives of history slighted the Dutch. The tiny Netherlands took on the giants of the Age of Absolutism, Philip II in Spain and Louis XIV in France; they extended the innovations of Italian

Renaissance capitalism and carried them further in the developments of banking and global capitalism. The relationship between the Netherlands and England—very much like that between the U.S.A. and Japan during and after World War II—is an intimate one in which war and finance interlock to restructure feudal kingdoms and transform them into modern industrial nation-states. The founding of the Bank of England after the Glorious Revolution is an expression of Dutch influence; it was modeled on the example of the Bank of Amsterdam. The massive investment of Dutch capital at the end of the seventeenth century and on into the early eighteenth century was essential in building up the infrastructure of roads and canals in England that paved the way for the Industrial Revolution of the middle of the eighteenth century.[42]

As I was reading one history book after another in preparation for writing this curriculum, I was struck anew by the omnipresence of war. The Thirty Years' War (which was an Eighty Years' War for the Dutch), the Anglo-Dutch War, the English Civil War, the Glorious Revolution, the War of the Spanish Succession, the Seven Years' War, the War of the Austrian Succession, the American Revolution, the French Revolution, the Napoleonic Wars, the War of 1812, the Latin American Wars of Liberation, the July Revolution, the Mexican-American War, the Revolutions of 1848, all of which are followed by the Crimean War, the American Civil War, the Franco-Prussian War, and on and on into the world wars of the twentieth century.

As a cultural historian, I am not personally attracted to the kind of boys' history that focuses on "who killed whom when and with what?" but one simply cannot ignore this cultural phenomenon in favor of a girls' history that shifts one's focus to painting, music, and literature in order that the future homemaker can learn how to be a tasteful collector of pretty things.

Of course, humans have been at one another's throats in organized war ever since the shift from hunting and gathering to the accumulation of property with stock raising and the defended settlements of agriculture. What is peculiar to modern

warfare is an oxymoronic relationship between capital formation and the technological invention of forms of destruction.
The Anglo-Dutch wars' rivalry and cross-investment are as complex as the American-Japanese relations in our age, and Simon
Schama shows how the Dutch came into the greatness of their
seventeenth-century golden age in and through war. So to move
beyond the simplistic thinking, in which there are periods of
normalcy called "peace" unnaturally interrupted by "wars,"
one should endeavor to think in terms of complex dynamical
systems in which opponents interlock to create novel emergent
states. In modern capitalist warfare—as opposed to tribal and
medieval warfare—the economic forces of destruction never
become greater than the forces of economic construction and
capital accumulation.[43] With all this in mind, I would suggest
that the teacher prepare a unit on the theme of "War as an
Oxymoronic Means of Communication."

I doubt if most teenagers are up to reading any of Locke's
two *Treatises on Government*, so at this point some textbook
digestion of this material may be necessary. Short selections from
Lord Macaulay's *History of England* (available in a Penguin
Classic paperback) will serve here.

Neither the seventeenth-century Tories nor the eighteenth-
century French Physiocrats could appreciate the new Whig ideas
of economic value, in which a national debt increases the supply
of money available to businessmen for investment and economic
growth. The feudal Tories still thought that currency had to be
backed up with land, and that the national economy was the sum
total of the value of the rents on the total acres in the kingdom.
Macaulay's discussion of the foundation of the Bank of England
should serve to stimulate discussion among students about just
what constitutes the ground for economic value and exchange
in the new capitalistic society.[44]

November—The Picaresque

To bring a more subjective perspective into the tutorial discussions of economics and society, I would suggest that we
pass from a consideration of economics, capital, and society

to a reading of Aphra Behn's novel about slavery, *Oroonoco* (1688), and at least parts of Defoe's longer novel *Moll Flanders* (1722). The epic poem is the quintessential art form of a heroic class of knights, but the novel is the quintessential art form of modernism. It performs the archetypal story of movement through space, of the individual's growth of character and fortune. The picaresque narrative does not focus on the aristocratic hero of the epic, but the rogue, rascal, beggar, and whore. Certainly, this shift from the hero to the common man was prefigured in Chaucer's *Canterbury Tales,* but it was the new genre of the novel that expanded upon these ideas of the individual and his or her journey through time and space. *Moll Flanders* allows us to consider these themes of individuation—rags to riches, redemption through the feminine, and the journey to the New World. As an example of the picaresque novel, it allows us to look back to Descartes's *Discourse, Don Quixote,* and *Lazarillo de Tormes* to understand modernism as a shift from medieval visions of transcendent sacrality to bourgeois realism and materialism. Defoe can also set the stage for a later discussion of urbanization, poverty, and the novel in Dickens's *Hard Times* and Engels's *Condition of the Working Classes in England.*

A subjective look at the urban poor through the character of Moll Flanders will help us consider just how the poor arrived in London in the demographic shifts from the countryside to the city. A look at the Enclosure Acts and the Highland Clearances can help the student to understand that the so-called "Glorious Revolution" of Parliament is still an affair of landed gentlemen. They are a law unto themselves and can decide to define the medieval commons as the private property of the lord, nullifying all the old feudal obligations and social relationships of tenant and landlord. The Highland Clearances express a social transformation in which an English-speaking lord scrapes the land clean of Gaelic-speaking crofters so that they can be replaced more profitably with sheep to supply the new industrial mills of the south. Emigration to the New World and to the cities of Lancaster, Birmingham, and Manchester is the result.[45]

December—The Enlightenment from Locke to Voltaire and Rousseau

The elimination of the medieval commons by the landlord class calls into question the whole relationship of the individual to the polity, and philosophers also respond to the dissolution of *noblesse oblige* by rethinking the social contract. At this point, I would consider the intellectual stirrings of the Enlightenment in Voltaire's *Letters on England* (1734), especially Letters 8, 9, 10, and 13, on Parliament, government, commerce, and Locke. One could read Voltaire's *Candide* as looking back to the philosophy of Leibniz—the contrast between the ebullience of a commitment to reason and the new misery of poverty. And one could examine the use of the New World as a space for the imagination by both Voltaire and Defoe. From Voltaire, I would move on to selections from Rousseau's *Social Contract* (1762), tying in his redefinitions of the individual and society with Defoe's and with the Parliamentary redefinitions of the Enclosure Acts (1760–1835). The rise of the philosophical tract and the novel in this new culture of the writer with its larger literate, middle-class public—as exemplified by Voltaire and Rousseau—provides us with another occasion to consider the role of media in society.

January—The British Takeover of India and the Loss of Her American Colonies

No sooner do the Moghuls consolidate their hold on Hindu India than the Europeans appear and begin to compete for control of the subcontinent in the game of empires. In January of 1757, Clive drives the French from India. In 1759, the French lose Quebec to the English. These losses will motivate the French to aid the Americans in their revolt against the British, and the Native Americans to continue the fight against their dispossession on their own in Pontiac's War (1763). An enlightened way of coming at this moment of history is to consider the American Revolution in the light of eighteenth-century geopolitics and the Enlightenment itself.

For a "unit" that unites the study of the Enlightenment and
the nature of the individual, I would suggest that the student
do an in-depth study of Thomas Jefferson. Jefferson, the monumental figure and avatar of freedom, is now undergoing a
deconstruction of his place as a heroic figure, so a consideration
of "the Great Man" and all his contradictions as slaveholder
and man of hidden passions will be timely. Concealment of the
self through a public narrative is also a pattern expressed in the
life and work of Rousseau—who hid his nonmarital relationship
and abandoned all his natural children to the orphanage—so a
unit on "print, privacy, revelation, and camouflage in the expression of the literary self in the Age of the Enlightenment" could
work very well here.

February—The Industrial Revolution of the 1780s in England

The bifurcation of European civilization involved what Henry
Adams called "an acceleration of history." Many things are
going on at once and interacting with one another in untraditional ways that traditional explanations, such as religion,
are no longer adequate to the task of keeping everyone and
everything tidily in place. The Financial Revolution is expanding the amount of capital available for trade and investment;
rivalry and national wars are encouraging maritime and military
innovations; expanding trade is creating markets for technological changes in the means of production; but factories require
economies of scale and global markets, so this locks in slavery
on cotton plantations to pauperization of workers in textile factories; and world wars like the Seven Years' War are interacting
with industrial revolution to create opportunities for France and
the American colonies to challenge England. Everything is going
on at once, so how the teacher moves back and forth between
the Enlightenment, the Industrial Revolution, the Seven Years'
War, the American Revolution, and the French Revolution will
be determined by her or his own intellectual understandings
and orientation. Intellectual historians will go from Locke to

Voltaire to Rousseau to Franklin and Jefferson. Economic historians will go from finance, interest rates, national debts, and bankruptcies to revolutions. For example, because England paid off its national debt at a lower interest rate than France, France's annual payments were double those of England's. Hence Paul Kennedy remarks: "The link between national bankruptcy and revolution was all too clear."[46] Monarchical France could not exploit its revenge against England in the American Revolution, but found its own feudal government collapsing in the throes of the French Revolution, while its defeated opponent England lurched forward from its failure to hold the American colonies to achieve global success in the technological transformations of the Industrial Revolution.

A good tie-in with literature for this section would be a reading of William Blake's *Songs of Innocence and Experience,* especially "London."[47] Maria Edgeworth's novella *Castle Rackrent* (1800) is a wonderful portrait of life at the edge between agricultural and industrial, and its sketches of landlord, agent, and peasant will help the student understand the Irish famine to come, as well as appreciate the obscure source for Faulkner's tales of Big House and hut, and all the other novels of the American South that were to follow.

March—The French Revolution and Its Influence

A close psychological study of Jefferson will also allow us to effect a narrative transition from the American to the French Revolution through a consideration of Jefferson's celebrations of violence and liberation, and his apology for French excesses. By taking a closer look at individuation and identity, we can prepare ourselves for the transition from revolutionary to emperor in the mythic figure of Napoleon. Our theme of individuation can address itself to self-mythologizing figures such as Napoleon, Toussaint L'Ouverture, and Simón Bolívar. Bolívar, like Thomas Jefferson, seems to be a larger-than-life figure whose contradictory invocations of liberation and a "war of extermination" reflect the complexity of a charismatic hero in the Napoleonic Era.[48] The evolution of the revolutionary personality into the authoritarian and imperial messianic figure seems to bring forward a romantic, nineteenth-century archetype that takes root in Latin America and lasts well into the twentieth century. A possible tie-in with literature would be to consider the Romantics. Mary Shelley's prophetic novel *Frankenstein* shows that this Promethean age is not only assaulting the fixed order of the Estates, but also the order of life and death itself. For teenagers who may think that rock stars invented bisexuality, a look at Lord Byron will be mind-expanding. In terms of media studies, Byron is interesting for his public life expresses the social evolution of the artist into the celebrity who both shocks and fascinates. Also, the death of Lord Byron fighting the Turk may be the world's first case of celebrity death. In the case of Percy Shelley (or Schiller for that matter), Romantic poetry expresses a Neoplatonic longing to escape time in a great leap into Eternity. One polarity of the magnetic field of the era is oriented to war and the new global economy of war as a dynamical system of constructing destruction; the other polarity is drawn to a ballistic leap into Eternity and intellectual Beauty. Whether through romantic violence in revolution or economic violence in war, the age is one of extreme light and shadow.

April—Action and Reaction, Counter-Revolution and Revolution Yet Again

Just as the Inquisition expressed a reaction to the Renaissance, so the Congress of Vienna and Metternich's efforts to stabilize Europe in a concert of nations express the aristocratic effort to undo the damage of the French Revolution. But the revolutionary spirit does not disappear. In fact it grows into a new spirit with the rise of romantic nationalism, whether it is the Greek struggle for independence from the Turks or the revolutions in Latin America. This is also the period in which feminism and the appeal for women's suffrage surfaces as part of a general articulation of human rights. One could reflect back to Mary Wollstonecraft's *Vindication of the Rights of Women* (1792), then consider William Thompson's 1825 work *An Appeal on One Half of the Human Race, Women, Against the Pretensions of the Other Half, Men, to Retain Them in Political and Hence Civil and Domestic Slavery.* Reaction is not able to hold society in traditional forms, and the failure of the Bourbon Restoration in France leads to the July Revolution in 1830.

May—Class Warfare and the Revolutions of 1848

Class warfare resurfaces in the Chartist Movement in England and in the struggles of the "hungry forties" when the conflicts between free trade and protectionism centered around the debates over the Corn Laws. The Irish Famine introduces the new politics of triage, in which the economy of property is protected at the cost of the lives of the propertyless. Here I would suggest a reading of Dickens's *Hard Times* and selections from Engels's *Condition of the Working Classes* in England as a general background for the revolutions of 1848 and the extension of suffrage to the nonpropertied classes in Switzerland and England. (Switzerland is one of the few countries in Europe where liberal revolution succeeds, and expresses the triumph of the middle class against Metternichian reaction.) To cover all this material, it will be necessary to focus more on structure and process than content and data, so one way to consider all the events from 1815 to 1848 is to focus on the dynamics of class struggle and warfare, such as peasant revolts and bandit leaders in nationalist Greece, aristocrats in Austria trying to push back the advances of the middle class, working classes in England in the Chartist movement, the petit bourgeoisie at the barricades in Paris, and a successfully revolutionary and liberal business class in Alfred Escher's Zurich of 1848. The month's study of class conflict and class warfare can profitably end with a reading of Karl Marx's *Communist Manifesto,* and perhaps one or two of the *Economical and Philosophical Manuscripts* that present the new hermeneutics of the "sociology of knowledge" as a way of reading society.

June—The Triumph of Industrial Society

After "the hungry forties" and the failures of the 1848 revolutions in France and Germany, both England and France regroup in a new celebration of the culture of wealth and industrial society. With the Crystal Palace and the Great Exhibition of London in 1851, which comes just three years after the Irish famine, England moves on into a global presentation of itself in the new technological euphoria—a mood not unlike our recent celebration of Internet technologies, e-commerce, and the World Wide Web. Exiled to England, Louis Napoleon is profoundly impressed by this nation and by London as a capital city. He returns to France and in a coup d'état establishes himself as "Prince-President." He appoints Baron Haussmann as Prefect of Paris and makes him responsible for the capital's complete reconstruction. The medieval quarters and shantytowns of the poor are replaced by broad boulevards along which troops can move swiftly to suppress insurrection and by high monuments that can celebrate the power and cultural authority of the centralized state and the capitalist upper-middle class. Out of these violent waves of revolution and reaction, destruction and reconsolidation, a new kind of industrial nation-state emerges and a new class of leaders addresses itself forcefully to the new global economy.

Some Suggested Threads
for Interweaving Grades Nine, Ten, and Eleven

1. War as an Oxymoronic Organization

Following up on the tenth grade's study of war as a construction of destruction that, paradoxically, does not destroy its own structure but does generate transcultural exchanges, we can reflect on the Anglo-Dutch conflicts of the seventeenth century. In this era, conflict, competition, and transnational investment brought about a shift of the economic capital of Europe from Amsterdam to London, and Dutch capital provided much of the investments that enabled Britain to construct the roads and canals that facilitated its Industrial Revolution. In much the same way, the American and Japanese competition and conflict in the Pacific interlocked the two nation-states and brought about the emergence of a new postwar global economy in which the bulk of American trade shifted from Europe to the Pacific Rim.

2. The Role of the World-City in the Development of Civilization

In the tenth grade, we looked at London as a world-city that celebrated a new consciousness of itself in the Crystal Palace and the Great Exhibition of 1851. When Walter Benjamin described Paris as "the capital city of the nineteenth century," he was, as a cultural critic, thinking more of architecture, art, literature, and science than economics and industry. This shift in the definition of civilization from industrial infrastructure to ideological suprastructure is empowered by the new world-city, an ecology of consciousness in which people do not simply share an ideology but participate in a culture in which architecture, painting, photography, poetry, technologies of transport and communication, novels, and works of science all interact in a process of emergence. This "civilization" of the nineteenth and twentieth centuries is decidedly novel and not simply a growth in size of the "civilization" of the seventeenth century.

Suggested "Units" for Integrated Studies

1. Following up on my suggestion that we consider Descartes's *Discourse on Method* as a picaresque narrative in which the soldier of fortune momentarily escapes the horrors of war and reflects on the role of human error in the search for truth, I suggest that for our thread on war, we consider the expressions of World War I in the war lyrics such as Wilfrid Owen's "Dulce et Decorum Est," or Virginia Woolf's study of shell shock and polite society in *Mrs. Dalloway.* The interiorization of the personal stream of consciousness, in both Woolf and James Joyce, is certainly one manner in which the globalization of space is contributing to a compensatory interiorization of identity and time. The collapse of confident bourgeois values in the postwar malaise also sees the rise of the artist as prophet, challenging both politician and priest. Joyce's *Portrait of the Artist as a Young Man*

is certainly a new testament in which the artist can declare: "I shall forge in the smithy of my soul the uncreated conscience of my race."

2. One of our threads stitching together grades nine, ten, and eleven can be "Economies of Addiction." Since drug use is a life-and-death choice that confronts teenagers, a historical study of this problem should get them where they live. Our year begins with the Opium Wars, in which England sought to balance its craving for tea by selling opium to the Chinese—this to avoid the enormous balance of payments problem caused by the Chinese refusal to buy mass-produced English factory "goods" and their insistence on payment in gold. The Opium War provides us with an occasion to reflect back on the relationship between sugar and slavery in the plantations of the seventeenth- and eighteenth-century economies, and look forward to the manner in which our contemporary American economy is structured on tobacco use and conflict with Latin America concerning the growth of coca and cannabis. Recent debates about the medicinal use of cannabis and the horrendous social costs of considering alcohol and tobacco as socially acceptable provide an occasion to reflect on the social construction of an interdicted substance.

3. To build upon the tenth grade's studies of opera and Mozart's *Magic Flute*, I suggest we study the architectural statement of the Paris Opera and, perhaps, Puccini's *Tosca* as a meditation on love and death, reaction and revolution.

4. As a tie-in with literature, I suggest a reading of Joseph Conrad's *Heart of Darkness* as a study of imperialism and the shadow-side of the civilizational process that is our major focus for the year. For an urban study of Haussmann's Paris, we can look at poems about the city, such as Baudelaire's *"Le cygne,"* or Paul Verlaine's *"La bonne chanson,"* in which he speaks of *"Le bruit des cabarets, la fange des trottoirs,"* or Rimbaud's *"L'orgie Parisienne ou Paris se repeuple."*

5. Another possible unit is to study the nature of perception in both painting and photography, looking at Monet and Atget, and what each has to say about the social consciousness of

urbanization in the Paris of the second half of the nineteenth century.

6. A unit in which mathematics, engineering, and architectural history can throw light on modern architecture could involve the examination of the structure and values of a particular building. I would suggest a comparative approach that analyzes the Crystal Palace of London, the Paris Opera, the Eiffel Tower, and the railroad station—the Gare Saint-Lazare—as the new technological cathedrals.

7. One of the threads for the entire eleventh grade is the nativistic or millenarian movement. It might prove interesting to the student to contrast contemporary fads of channeling and millennial prophecy with those involved in the Taiping Rebellion or the Ghost Dance. The study of these millenarian movements gives us a chance to introduce psychological ideas through the character analysis of a prophetic leader, a Hung Hsiu-ch'uän or a Louis Riel.[49]

Suggested Tie-ins with Science

Theme: Evolution and the transformation of life and consciousness: elements taken from biology, genetics, thermodynamics, psychology, biochemistry, neurophysiology, and cognitive science.

The transformation of the understanding of time through the reading of fossils and geological landscapes leads to new theories of development, culminating in Darwinian evolution and the birth of the new science of genetics with Gregor Mendel and William Bateson. This wedding of an expanded conception of space to an expanded sense of time leads to an experience of acceleration of space wed to time in a process of modernization that transforms industrial civilization and creates a break between modernizing and traditional societies. New institutions like the École Polytechnique and MIT are created and become the driving engines for the emergence of the modern industrial nation-state. Evolution as the narrative of time becomes conscious of itself, and its first articulation is in imperialism, an ideology that sees savagery at one end of the continuum in the Belgian Congo and European science and civilization at the other. With the articulation of the "stream of consciousness" by William James, and of the unconscious by Freud, the nature of consciousness becomes the new wilderness subject to scientific invasion, first with psychology and psychoanalysis, then with psychopharmacology, and then with cybernetics and artificial intelligence and artificial life. The brain becomes the new forest of neurons, inciting both clear-cutting in the case of the eliminativism of the Churchlands, and ecological retrieval in the case of the Enactivism of Francisco Varela and Evan Thompson.[50] In the new sciences of complexity, a new meta-narrative begins to emerge that involves the evolution of the cell, the emergence of planetary biological autonomy ("Gaia"), and the emergence of intelligent machines as homeomorphic performances of complex dynamical systems.

The Eleventh Grade

Theme: Global economic consolidation and visionary revolts (1850–2001).

Theory: In the ninth grade, the archetypal idea is space, the expansion and articulation into the new world space in the voyages of discovery. In the tenth grade, the archetypal idea was Time, the story of the individual's rise from rags to riches, from Old World to New, from oppression to revolutionary liberation. In the eleventh grade, the archetypal ideas are speed and transformation—the wedding of time to space in the acceleration of culture in modernization through the instrumentalities of the new cultural vehicles of the world-city and the world war. In both of these, the new transportational vehicles of railroad, automobile, truck, tank, airplane, jet, and rocket have enormous impact on traditional cultures and religious worldviews, which react to modernization with visionary movements of mythopoeic prophecy and fundamentalist resacralization. The conflict between the mechanists and the mystics in the articulation of values for a new world civilization continues to this day.

Practice: The explication of the relationships between art, mathematics, and science in configurations such as Cubism and special relativity, or chaos dynamics in Poincaré and Kupka, as well as the relationships between media such as photography, cinema, painting, and the construction of the past in Haussmann's urban planning, Bergson's philosophy of memory, and Proust's recapture of past time.

Integrative Studies Project: Nativistic movements and the psychology of the prophetic leader; Paris and the reconstruction of past time. Chaos dynamics in math, music, and painting: the example of Poincaré-Satie-Kupka.

September—Global Economic Consolidation and Visionary Revolt

The Opium Wars, the forceful "opening" of China, and the Taiping Revolt should be studied as the archetype of the nativistic movement, in which the mystics reject the threat of technological innovation and seek to "resacralize" culture in a visionary revolution in which top becomes bottom and bottom becomes top. These millennial and nativistic movements attempt to counter the global consolidation of space in the world economy with an interiorization and mythic resacralization of time and identity.

October—Modernization Versus Traditional Civilization

1. The Meiji restoration in Japan (1853). The forceful opening of Japan by the American navy compared to the forceful opening of China by the British during the Opium Wars. The impact of the West on Japan and the reconstruction of traditional Japanese society.

2. Haussmann's reconstruction of medieval Paris.[51] Parallel to the Meiji reconstruction of medieval Japan is Louis Napoleon

and Baron Haussmann's reconstruction of medieval Paris. What is brought forth is a new landscape of the city as a perspectival monument in which the Middle Ages are erased and a new past is "constructed"—an urban theme park of patriotism and national glory in which the aristocratic past becomes the backdrop for a new and radically bourgeois present of luxury apartments.

As a broadening of this study of social conflict in the clash of traditional and industrial societies, one can consider the class warfare of the Paris Commune (1871). When the Communards shoot the hands off the clocks in Paris, there is a millenarian aspect to their sense that they have reached the end time of an apocalypse and a new world order. The violent massacres of the poor in East Paris show that the juggernaut that is rolling over the lower classes, whether in Paris or Ireland, is not all that different from the collision of cultures occurring in the conquest of the American West and South Africa.

Coeval with this urban and middle-class transformation of the city is a new articulation of the role of nostalgia and memory in the formation of human identity in the works of Bergson and Proust and in early photographers of the city such as Marville and Atget. The train station now becomes the new cathedral that celebrates the new collective ritual of speed and movement.[52] The city itself becomes a vehicle of human cultural evolution, and "Paris" as a complex dynamical system of bankers and architects, poets and painters, scientists and philosophers becomes the preeminent cultural world-city for the new global economy of the Gold Standard of the last third of the nineteenth century.[53]

November

3. The American Civil War. The consolidation of the industrial nation-state, the rise of the imperial presidency under Lincoln; the industrialization of warfare and its consequent deprofessionalization as foot soldier replaces warrior and civilian populations become victimized and integrated into the theater of war. Here Gore Vidal's novel *Lincoln* is a good antidote to the Lincoln hagiography on which I was raised.

4. The railroad and telegraph and the expansion of the United States into a continental industrial nation-state. The military conquest of the Native American peoples.

5. The mystics versus the mechanists. The Ghost Dance (1870–1890) in the United States and Louis Riel's revolt of the métis in Canada (1869–1885) are examples of nativistic movements in which religious vision challenges technological and economic consolidation. A global approach to the conflict between imperialistic and nativistic movements can be emphasized by noting that the Canadian Mounted Police that is used to suppress the revolt of the métis was modeled upon the "Peelers," the police force created by the English to control the Irish. The "Land War" of the Irish against the English is another example of the collision of cultures, and the dependency of Gladstone upon the votes of the Irish MPs placed a check upon Britain's imperial expansion into Africa.[54]

December

6. The climax of imperialism and the appropriation of Africa (1876–1902). The high medieval civilizations of Africa had been successfully able to resist European conquest, but under the impact of the nineteenth-century European industrial revolution and expansion, Africa begins to cave in and is carved into colonies for the imperialist states of Western Europe. The Anglo-Zulu War of 1879 parallels the American Indian wars in the United States, and the prophetic movement of the Mahdi (1881–98) in the Sudan parallels the Ghost Dance in America. On both continents, tribe confronts empire in a conflict between mystics and mechanists, a conflict in which the resacralization of space and time conflicts with the mechanization of space and time in the world market. It will be important for the student to realize that these nineteenth-century conflicts, such as that between General Gordon and the Mahdi, are still taking place around the world. The Islamic fundamentalist movements that the technological West labels "terrorism," the traditionalist Middle East calls holy war or *jihad*.

January—The Revisioning of Time and Space in the New Global Civilization: The Climax of Materialistic Imperialism and the Paradoxical Disintegration of Victorian Materialism in the Emergence of Modernism

The scientific-materialist image of space as an empty void in which forces and bodies move and collide generates a new world space in which industrial nation-states expand and then collide with one another, e.g., Britain, the U.S., Germany, France, and Russia. The Darwinian revisioning of sacral time also generates a new vision of evolution and progress in which it is the Manifest Destiny of the white race to overwhelm and lead the darker peoples of the Earth. Racism becomes the apologetics for a new system of domination, a mythology of progress in which historical time becomes the lifting up of the chosen elect. The sluggards who resist this technological apotheosis become demonized as "barbarians" and "savages." The ideal vision is revealed in the statue at the entrance to New York's Museum of Natural History: Teddy Roosevelt is the white man on a horse, leading humanity into a future in which the red man, the barbarian, and the black man, the savage, follow dutifully on foot.

This new process of globalization in the industrial marketplace no longer requires agricultural slavery for its foundation, but it does require a system of collectivization in which the laboring classes are seen as the internal "other," an internal source of unrest and barbarism. From the Enclosure Acts to the Highland Clearances to the Irish Famine to the American Indian wars to the Paris Commune, the way of progress had been consistently advanced in the shift from medieval to modern. Those who stand in the way of progress are not seen as philosophers, but as subhuman vestiges of a dark age. In London, the illustrated newspapers caricature the Irish as apes and degenerate humans, as "the missing link" of evolution. In America, the Irish struggle to escape their racist classification by becoming "white" and shifting the finger to the Afro-American as the real "nigger" of immigrant America.[55] This demonization, first extended to the Irish by Cromwell in the seventeenth century, is extended to the Native American peoples, then the Mexicans, the Chinese, and any nonwhite peoples, be they Hawaiian or Filipino. This racist imperialism reaches its peak in the Spanish-American War and the American takeover of Hawaii and the Philippines. But this expansion of the industrial nation-states means that sooner or later, as America, Asia, and Africa have been appropriated into the new world economy, the new industrial nation-states will collide with one another. In the Russo-Japanese War (1904–1905), Japan seeks to stop European expansion, but Theodore Roosevelt moves in to broker a peace so as to place the United States in the position of the architect as the new world space of the Pacific Rim.

February

As the smug confidence of the economic leaders of imperialism moves towards its dénouement in World War I, the intellectuals begin to undermine materialism in the cultural formation we now call modernism. With the articulation of the unconscious with Freud (*Studies in Hysteria*, 1895), and Poincaré's revelation of the chaotic behavior of the solar system in 1899, followed by quantum mechanics with Max Planck (1902), Cubism with Braque and Picasso (1904) and Special Relativity with Einstein (1905),[56] the confident world of the Victorians collapses and its national fragments crash into one another in the First World War.

March, April, and May—World Wars and Nativistic Revolts

In order not to drown in an ocean of data as one endeavors to present World War I, the Irish, Mexican, and Russian Revolutions, the Depression, World War II, Indian Independence, the Chinese Revolution, the Korean War, African and Asian decolonization, the Cuban Revolution, the Vietnam War, the countercultural explosions of 1967–68, the electronic globalization of the economy, the breakup of the Soviet Empire, the Gulf War, and the explosion of a Serbian nativistic movement

based upon blood identity, sacralized space, and a violent demonization of the "Other," I suggest we move up to a more
satellite-like vision of the events on planet Earth from 1914
to the present. A historian focusing on Africa and Asia concentrates on the rise and fall of the Western Empires and the
era of colonial liberation and wars of national independence. A
historian focusing on war and revolutions concentrates on the
battles of World Wars I and II and the Russian and Chinese
Revolutions. An anthropologist focusing on nativistic, millenarian, and revolutionary movements will take the approach I have
suggested. A historian in urban studies or economic history will
concentrate on the development of the city and the new global
economy. Of course, all of the above things were happening at
the same time.

But in the interest of fashioning a coherent narrative for this
global mass of material, I propose that we see the period as
expressing two opposed and countervailing forces. The *yang*
vortex of this global Lorenz dynamical attractor is a centrifugal
force moving outward in military and economic competition for
global resources fundamental to technological superiority. Thus,
when Churchill shifts the British Admiralty from coal-fired ships
to lighter and faster oil-driven fleets, England can no longer depend on its own national supplies of coal, but must look to the
Middle East and Indonesia for oil. This oil-generated increase
in speed for navies is also duplicated in the new personal vehicle of the automobile, and so the "rubber meets the road" in
a new demand for Malaysian resources. Suddenly, Japan Inc.,
Anglo-Dutch Petroleum, and Standard Oil find themselves in a
struggle for control of the global resources upon which their national economies depend in Malaysia, Indonesia, and the Middle
East. The projection of economic power is thus linked to a world
navy, and World Wars I and II are really chapters in a single
story. Central to this story, however, is a social evolution in
which science and technology bring into being a new "national
security state" of nuclear weapons and secret management.[57] In
compensation for this antipopulist movement, a new consumer
society is brought into being, as credit is extended to the working

classes and suburban society expands. Through the new culture of television, from Senator McCarthy to President Kennedy,
government becomes more a condition of informational management as elections become media events analogous to public
sports and entertainment.

The *yin* of this global dynamical attractor is an opposed and
countervailing force, a centripetal movement toward inner identity and mythologized locality. Most often this force sets itself in
opposition to the extroverted forces of the global economy by
going back to the preindustrial economy in a mythological resacralization of the peasant. The Irish and Mexican Revolutions
led by Padraic Pearse and Emiliano Zapata are clear examples
of this, but so is Lenin's mystification of the peasant and the
factory worker, or Gandhi's mythological celebration of cottage
industries and the spinning wheel. Jomo Kenyata's expulsion of
the White Man and his celebration of the nativistic values of the
Kikuyu tribesmen are similar to Pearse's rejection of the *Sasse-
nach* and his idealization of the Gaeltacht peasant. And on it
goes, from one end of the twentieth century to the other, from
Pearse to Mao and Castro's idealized peasantry encircling the
decadent cities of capitalism and corruption.

Elements of nativistic movements can also be combined in
the formation of political ideologies for industrial societies. Germany, after the Treaty of Versailles, felt that its culture was at
the edge of extinction. This fear exploded in the nativistic movement of National Socialism, with its hatred of foreigners, its
demonization of the Jews, and its mythologizing of *das Volk* in
a nativist vision of *Blut und Boden*. As World War II progressed,
Nazi Germany's mythology served as camouflage for more ordinary forms of capitalist expansion for its large corporations and
their need to secure natural resources for their continued growth.
These contradictions between nationalism and global capitalism are nicely caricatured in Thomas Pynchon's award-winning
novel, *Gravity's Rainbow,* and are now resurfacing in the examination of the role of General Motors and its German affiliates in
Nazi Germany. How the mythologies of Cuchulain and Siegfried
compare and contrast in the cases of the Irish Revolt of 1916

and the National Socialist movement in Germany would itself make an interesting study of the roles of myth and media in the construction of national identity.

June—Conclusion and Recapitulation of the Entire Curriculum: The World-City and the Emergence of Planetary Culture

The city is not simply a location in space, but also a vehicle in time that can itself accelerate the evolution of consciousness. Like molecules packed into the membrane of a cell, the minds that are packed into a city take on a new life that is energized by the city's intensification of space and time.

The first cities of ancient Sumer were ceremonial centers organized around the sacred precinct of the temple. Sumerian mythology stated that these cities were founded and lived in by the gods. One of the earliest texts we have in Sumerian mythology is the story of how the goddess Inanna transferred the arts of civilization (the *me*'s) from the city of Eridu, favored by the god Enki, to her own beloved Erech. The text is a fundamental expression of the ancient Arithmetic Mentality, as it displays the numinosity of the list and delights in repeating, in strophe after strophe, the enumeration of these *me*'s that were loaded on and unloaded from Inanna's riverine barge.[58]

This ancient Sumerian poem enables us to see how both literature and mathematics participate in a historically dependent mentality in which a worldview is structured by a particular dynamical mode of perception and narration, be it Arithmetic (or Ancient), Geometrical (or Classical), Algebraic (or Medieval), Galilean Dynamical (or Renaissance/Modern), or Chaos-Dynamical (or Contemporary).

Within the sacred precinct, a steward, an *Ensi,* ruled over the ceremonial city for the absentee landlord of the god. Over the years, as the gods receded in the daily experience of humans, the day-to-day reality of human rulership became much more visible. We can see this social evolution of mystique into *politique* as a three-stage process in which the ceremonial center grows into the imperial city.

1. *The gods rule* (stage of the *Ensi*).
2. *I rule for the gods* (stage of shepherd-king).
3. *I rule!* (stage of the emperor).

Ancient cities around the world seem to begin as ceremonial centers, and then, through trade and warfare, grow into imperial centers. The early Sumerian cities and the Mesoamerican cities, San Lorenzo Tenochtitlán and Teotihuacán, are examples of the first type. Babylon, Persepolis, Peking, and Rome are examples of the second type. From Babylon to Peking to Rome, imperial cities were the general rule for planet Earth during the period of ancient, classical, and medieval civilizations. An empire would rise, extend its rule from court to provinces, until the point where there would be a reversal, and the outlying provinces would overrun the imperial city. The climax formation of this civilizational system of a periodic attractor, oscillating back and forth between civilization and barbarism, was seen in medieval societies like Ming China, pre-Columbian Mesoamerica, and the Islamic and Christian civilizations surrounding the Mediterranean basin.

In the cultural shift from an empire based on conquest and tribute to a polycentric world economy based on trade and finance with interest-generating loans, there arose a shift in perspective from the past to the future. Indebtedness has as its phase-space the future, so one naturally becomes interested in the time to come when one's ship will come in, one's loan will be paid off, and full payment will be made. The new kind of city that arose with this new world economy was the trading city—Florence, Genoa, and Venice at the beginning of the modern period, Antwerp and Amsterdam in the middle, and London and New York at the end.

With the expansion of trade and technology, artisans who found themselves in low esteem in aristocratic, feudal societies found themselves growing in independence and influence as they became the artists and scientists of an expanding industrializing society. A city that grew to become a capital for this new culture of art and science was late nineteenth-century

Paris. Indeed, for the social critic Walter Benjamin, Paris was the capital of civilization for the last third of the nineteenth century.[59] For the sake of heuristic playfulness, let us imagine that Paris 1851 to 1914 is a processual object, a phenomenology of culture bounded by a permeable membrane that is reflexive in time and reflective in space. The minds that live within this membrane begin to take on a collective mental behavior that is peculiar to them, and as they interact within this ethos or system of values, they begin to bring forth mental creations that seem to flourish within this particular domain of time and space. Like jazz musicians listening to one another's riffs before they take off on their own, Parisians are energizing other Parisians. Manet is listening to Mallarmé at the beginning of this period, and Kupka is listening to Poincaré at the end, but throughout this period from 1851 to 1914, all these creative thinkers are listening to Paris. Railways are influencing both Monet and Zola, and just as Haussmann's reconstruction of Paris destroyed medieval Paris in order to recreate a more conscious monument to a bourgeois vision of the past, Bergson in *Matière et mémoire* and Proust in *Du côté de chez Swann* also excavated the past in an exploration of the nature of memory as constitutive of human identity. This focusing on matter and its saturation with invested meaning is, of course, not unique to Proust and Bergson, but is at the heart of the capitalistic fixing of value on gold in the new global gold standard economy.[60] Interestingly enough, that most unrooted and wandering poet, Rainer Maria Rilke, is also concerned at this time with *Dinglichkeit*—but then Rilke too was in Paris and was secretary to Rodin, and Proust was one of the first to read and become enthusiastic about Rilke. Rilke was also quite influenced by Cézanne, so this new attention to the psychological nature of perception is something worth "looking at." To our thoughts of Manet and Monet, we must add a glance at the beginnings of photography with Marville and Atget, and then with cinema and the brothers Lumière, one begins to appreciate the manner in which city and media are beginning to play off one another.

All of that is not too far out, so let's take it a step further to suggest that what is helping to form the membrane of time and space, to give living structure to the evolutionary vehicle of Paris, has also to do with an economy as well as a technology, and a war as well as an explosion of artistic and scientific creativity. So let us imagine a table of correspondences:

	Paris	New York	Los Angeles
War	Franco-Prussian War, World War I	World War II	Cold War
Economy	Gold standard	"The Crash"	Nixon's post–Breton Woods floating exchange rates—a form of Derrida's *différance*
Technology	Railway	Mass transit, subway, and "El"	Automobile
Media	Painting, photography, and cinema	Radio and movies	Movies and TV
Temporal Mode	The past, historical monument	The Now; the skyscraper	The future and fantasy; freeways, theme parks
Dynamical Mentality	Poincaré	Macy conferences; information theory	Complex Dynamical Systems
Musical Mentality	Satie	Gershwin, Miles Davis, and "birth of the cool"	Music as acoustical architecture; informational economy
Archetypal Novel	Proust, *À la recherche du temps perdu*	Dos Passos, *Manhattan Transfer*	Pynchon, *The Crying of Lot 49*

To take it from the bottom: Satie, influenced by hearing Indonesian gamelan music at the Universal Exhibition of 1889 in Paris, and drawing on his own mystical Rosicrucian musings of 1891, eliminates temporal bar markings in his musical compositions and attempts to create a tonal extensiveness. This is a musical prefiguring of Bergson's 1896 analysis of time as *durée*. This dissolution of absolute mechanical clock time is echoed in Poincaré's discovery that the solar system is not an orderly mechanical clock, but a chaotic system. Kupka sits in on Poincaré's lectures, and in his paintings from 1911 on he begins to express fractal architectures, self-similarity, and collisions of laminar and chaotic flows.[61] In New York, street sounds in Gershwin, and jazz in general, begin to explore noise and "self-organization from noise" right about the time that the scientists in the Macy conferences—Bateson, von Neumann, and von Forster, as well as Shannon across the Hudson in Bell Telephone Labs in New Jersey—are all beginning to study self-organization from noise in cybernetics and information theory. In Los Angeles, the theme park as the fake city of Disneyland begins to use movie music as emotional crowd controls, with speakers in the monorail, the bushes, the lavatories, and restaurants.[62] Muzak in elevators and factories becomes an experiment with subliminal systems of social control, and pop music expands globally to become a new kind of collective architecture and currency of exchange in the informational economy, in which the pop star becomes a new kind of postindustrial tycoon.

In other words, what the moiré pattern of war, economy, media, artistic and scientific invention allows us to see is that minds are not discrete entities, but are embedded within an ecology of consciousness, and what the intellectual city like Paris brought forth in its artistic and scientific creations was the evolution of a new kind of noetic polity of synchronous emergence—one that has now been passed over in new forms of synchronous emergence in more global forms of cyberspace (although I would still rather live in the physically supported noetic polity of multicultural Manhattan than in the abstract cyberspace of a nerdy noetic polity supported from a computer terminal in white supremacist Idaho). Paris, as an urban artifact, certainly expressed an escape from nature, but its celebration of the glory of the past with its heroic monuments disguised this shift with a certain conservatism. But with the Eiffel Tower there was a reaching up to break free of nature that inspired New York's efforts to escape the ground of nature in the skyscrapers of the Flatiron Building, the Empire State Building, and Rockefeller Center. King Kong falling to his death from the Empire State Building expressed an almost archetypal death of the old nature in the new state of culture.

In Los Angeles, New York's polarization between tenement and penthouse is overcome in the flattened suburban megalopolis of the new postwar universal middle class. Here credit as an imaginary currency becomes the new ground of the economy, and fantasy becomes the new system of identity. The whole culture is literally indebted to the future, so the imagination of the future becomes the new fictional ground that supports value and identity. The great soldiers and scientists of Paris and the great millionaires of New York are replaced by the celebrity, a creature of pure image and illusion. In this new State of Entertainment, advertising replaces political philosophy and entertainment replaces education, so a presidential campaign becomes a consensual delusion and Reagan becomes the first Disney animatron president as celebrity, celebrity as president.

Three novels that embody the distinct *kairos* of their chosen cities are Proust's *À la recherche du temps perdu* for Paris, John Dos Passos's *Manhattan Transfer* for New York, and Thomas Pynchon's *Crying of Lot 49* for Los Angeles. With Proust, perception, memory, and the nature of time are part of a concern that is part of a vast Parisian thought-complex, one shared by Bergson, and the new media of photography and film. With Dos Passos, the writer performs self-consciously modernist fiction in the narrative techniques of collage and quick cuts of simultaneity that focus on the phase-space of the "now" and prefigure the narrative techniques that have taken over television storytelling, from "Hill Street Blues" to "E.R." With Pynchon, the chaotic informational overload of the megalopolis generates a new landscape of fantasy-identity, conspiracy theories, and paranoid reintegration. Paranoia as a mad system of informational integration is a shadow-formation that paradoxically throws light upon the shift from postindustrial to informational society. It is a caricature of the cultural transition from the world metropolis to the planetary noetic polity in which the territorial nation-state dissolves in visions of globalist associations.

Both nineteenth-century Paris and twentieth-century New York are examples of the city evolving from the materialistic and capitalistic city into the informational noetic polity, one in which an overlapping moiré of economic center, artistic center, and intellectual center creates a pattern in which no single institution is imperialistically in control. Thus an emergent state comes forth in which consciousness moves to a level above the traditional formations of an urban civilization. Since even this contemporary manifestation of megalopolitan growth now seems to be simply a node within the planetary informational lattice of the World Wide Web, it is hard to prophesy just where this contemporary noetic polity is taking us in cultural evolution.

My guess is that the coming etherealization of architecture through atomic nanotechnologies will enable one to turn buildings on and off like electric lights, but will continue to make cities like New York appealing nostalgic artifacts of previous states of cultural evolution, and like Haussmann's Paris, historical camouflage to their true but more invisible structure. Los Angeles, in contrast to New York, is a single-industry city, that industry being entertainment—movies, television, and theme parks. (Both Disneyland and Las Vegas are basically theme park suburbs of L.A.) From my perspective, L.A. is isomorphic to the Vatican, and is the Vatican of our new State of Entertainment, in which politicians, sports figures, movie stars, and celebrities are all the potentates of the new willfully deluded polity. Cambridge, Massachusetts, is also a single-industry city, and that is what makes it less interesting than New York. Creative artists who earn their keep as professors at Harvard, MIT, Tufts, or Boston often get bored with their unimaginative academic colleagues and move to New York as soon as their income allows them to break loose from tenured servitude to the monocrop noetic polity of the university.

New York is not a single-industry city, and that is what makes it so much more interesting than commercial Zurich or even contemporary Paris. Contemporary Paris has more of a conformist and collective manner to its intellectual style of life, but New York is so vast that one can live and write here and never have to run into or conform to the styles of Susan Sontag or Norman Mailer. New York is a kind of mitochondrion of Archaean evolution that has moved into some gigantic Gaian planetary cell for the next stage in evolution. The moiré pattern that emerges from the overlap of Wall Street, the United Nations, music and performing arts, publishing, and universities makes it as interesting now as Paris must have been in the time of Proust, Bergson, and Poincaré.

In the interval between World Wars I and II, the global economy contracted and restructured itself as the capital of the world economy shifted from London to New York. This restructuring is called the Great Depression,[63] and in his efforts to save American capitalism, FDR was not fully successful until he put America on a wartime economy. This extension of credit to the manufacturers was continued through the extension of the war into the Cold War, with its stimulation of the new aerospace industries. This new postindustrial economy was created by massive intrusion of Big Government into the private sector, but almost by accident, in the case of the GI Bill, the United States government stumbled upon the idea of extending credit to consumers and not just factory producers, and these new forms of support for higher education and the purchase of homes shaped the new world of the suburbs in the Baby Boom. When the National Defense Act put the construction of the Interstate Highway system on the federal tab as well, the wedding of suburban tracts to highways created the new culture of the automobile and the shopping mall. With a continuing extension of credit and indebtedness to consumers, credit cards, television, movies, and theme park images of history all interacted to bring forth a whole new postindustrial society.

In a 1945 essay, "The Planetization of Mankind," Teilhard de Chardin observed:

Every new war, embarked upon by the nations for the purpose of detaching themselves from one another, merely results in their being bound and mingled together in a more inextricable knot. The more we seek to thrust each other away, the more do we interpenetrate.[64]

And so after World War II, Detroit automotive factories end up in Japan and Japanese Zen Buddhist monasteries end up in California.

In the countercultural movements of 1968, these *yin* and *yang* forces collided in America and Western Europe and brought both France and the United States to the edge of civil war. In industrial society, the displaced agricultural laborers were gathered into factories, looked at one another and recognized themselves as the new working class. In the informational society of the age of television, the young were collectivized in suburbs and public universities—in the generation gap—and looked around and recognized themselves as the new counterculture. In the Vietnam War, the United States sought to extend the colonial policies of the French and contain Chinese expansion by controlling Japan's economic dependency on Malaysian and Indonesian oil and resources, and thus the U.S. expressed the *yang* force in a straightforward manner. But the informational proletariat of the young in the U.S. and Western Europe exploded in a new expression of identity, interiority, and mystification of a romantic past in the back-to-the-Earth commune and hippie costume. "Folk" music was electronically retrieved through the figures of Joan Baez and Bob Dylan, and the Depression of Woody Guthrie became a pastoral artifact in the affluent consumer culture of the sixties.

This first wave of the counterculture of the postindustrial society of the 1960s expressed a revolutionary and Dionysian consciousness in a mystical shift from the territorial nation-state to the "extraterrestrial" noetic polity, and this found public artistic expression in drugs, global pop music, and many works of popular science fiction concerned with visions of extraterrestrial invasion.

The second wave of the counterculture that came out of Silicon Valley in California in the 1980s expressed a more Apollonian consciousness of reembodiment in new informational corporations and new forms of artificial intelligence. Here we saw a shift from the consciousness of an autonomous self within a biological evolutionary body to more distributive lattices of multidimensional mind, in which new media constellated new forms of the extensive phase-space of consciousness through personal computers, the Internet, and the World Wide Web. Thus in the exchange of opposites characteristic of conflict as well as diploid sexual reproduction, the exteriority of the *yang* force crosses with the interiority of the *yin* force in a form of planetary cellular mitosis that seems about to give birth to a new kind of life in which natural and artificial are more intimately bound together in artificial life and electronic organisms.

In this emergence of the novel state of cultural evolution, the old condition is used as a nostalgic camouflage-content for the structure. Notice that the ideology of capitalism in the United States is filled with the imagery of family values, evangelical Protestantism, and rugged individualism: all of which are opposite to the cultural drift of the economic processes Republicans energize. In much the same way, Paris in the nineteenth century began by focusing on matter and the past in the photography of Atget, the perspectival monumentality of Haussmann, and the excavations of memory in Bergson and Proust, but ended up in a new nonobjective state of consciousness in Poincaré and Kupka, and, of course, in the aperspectival Cubism of Braque and Picasso. Twentieth-century New York started out as an escape from the past into a modernist Now, but ended up as a hierarchical and highly concretized city as artifact of the corporate past. Postwar Los Angeles started out as the vast extensive and flattened city of the new universal middle class, but ended up as an informational lattice in which nodes such as Las Vegas, Silicon Valley, and Santa Fe became like urban metastases. Our new planetary noetic polity does not seem to be a city fixed to a physical location, so the giantism of Los Angeles now serves as a content-camouflage to its rather monistic uniformity in a consciousness that is locked on to the State of Entertainment, much as New York in the fifties and sixties was locked onto the corporatism of its aluminum and glass skyscrapers around Rockefeller Center.

Before the outbreak of World War I, psychoanalysis, quantum mechanics, Cubism, and special relativity began to express an intellectual shift away from the pious certainties of the materialist bourgeois worldview. In 1972, a new planetary culture began to express itself in contradistinction to the internationalism that had been dominant in the era of World War II and the Cold War. James Lovelock published his first paper on the Gaia Theory that expressed a new way of looking at planetary dynamics, and Jay Forester and the Meadows at MIT published their first efforts at understanding the relationship between the global economy and the global ecology in *Limits to Growth*. New forms of mathematics, first in catastrophe theory and then in chaos dynamics, began to express the shift from linear systems of cause and effect to emergent states and complex dynamical systems. The politics of nation-states are still struggling to understand this cultural transformation in which the interiority of the *yin* force expresses itself in the planetization of the esoteric in popular movements of mysticism and meditation, while the *yang* force expresses itself in a global economy of GATT and NAFTA. As the ozone hole and the Greenhouse Effect begin to transform global weather patterns, the relationship between the global economy and the global ecology is becoming more apparent, and also, quite apparently, is not under the control of the globalist managers. We can call this shift from a collection of competing industrial nation-states to a planetary culture, the shift from a global economy (Clinton-Gore-Bush et al.) to a planetary *ecumene*.

Like the ancient city-states of Sumer that were united by rivers, the new cities along the Pacific Rim seem to be part of an emergent structure that is neither simply a culture nor an economy, but something like the molecular soup that prefigured the evolution of cells. The infectious case of Los Angeles certainly seems to be a model for these new global cities of the Pacific Rim, "the new Mediterranean." With more than eighty languages in its public schools, L.A. is no longer simply an "American" city. It is First World and Third World at the same time, but having grown up there as a teenager, I prefer to live as an old man in New York.

Perhaps we are experiencing a shift from a world economy of competing and polluting industrial nation-states to a global ecology of noetic polities in which consciousness will become a symbiotic architecture of organisms and machines, one in which pollution is mined as a natural resource in a cultured bacterial technology and a complex ecology of "living machines" and electronic organisms.[65] Certainly, to track and describe this new emergent state, we shall need the narratives of complex dynamical systems. Perhaps here science fact and science fiction are coming together to open our imaginations to the future and the possibilities of multidimensional modes of consciousness that can be both mystical and mathematical.

Note on Textbooks

Textbooks, CD-ROMs, and Web sites change from year to year. A parent can find what textbooks are available for children by contacting or browsing through a bookstore for children associated with a school of education, such as the Bank Street Bookstore in New York. For human evolution, there is the Expert Software's CD-ROM, *Evolution of Man* (ISBN 1-57709-680-0), *support@expertsoftware.com*. The *Usborne World History: Ancient World* is a good one for children, and Usborne has a whole series of texts, such as *Who Were the First People?* Oxford also has a series of texts, such as *First Ancient History*, but this text is rather Eurocentric, with only two pages on China. Marion Wood's *Ancient America* (Oxford, 1990) is a useful overview. As a home library reference set for parents, or young adults, there is the twenty-five-volume *TimeFrame* from Time Life Books in Alexandria, Virginia. To ensure that parents and students both have a *diachronic* sense of history as well as a *synchronic* sense of the space of global culture, I recommend that *The Kingfisher Illustrated History of the World*, edited by Jack Zevin (New York: Larousse Kingfisher Chambers, 1993), be used as a common reference book for parents and students from ages five through thirteen, and the historical atlas, the *Times Illustrated History of the World*, edited by Geoffrey Barraclough (London: Times Books, 1999), for ages thirteen to sixteen.

Caveat on Teaching History
As a Linear Narrative of Progress

Although this narrative of history is concerned with tracking emergent states of cultural development, it is important to keep in mind that one mathematical-literary mentality is not necessarily more moral than another. I can imagine circumstances where one might wish to say that this traditional culture is more moral than this technological culture. To make certain that this outline of development from hominization of the primates to the planetization of humanity does not become a simple linear narrative of Whig history triumphalism, it would be better to think in terms of development as a dialectical one of political consolidation linked with a consequent cultural displacement.

As a metaphor of this process, think of the evolution of the cell with a nucleus, the eukaryotic cell. The tiny mitochondrion is engulfed by the giant cell. Presumably at one time the larger cell was interested in "eating" it. But the organelle's membrane held intact, and the giant cell found that the respiration of the mitochondrion allowed it to generate the ATP cycle it needed for the higher energy budget of its gigantic life. This new internal form of respiration also allowed new cellular processes to emerge, such as sexual reproduction in mitosis. So there was a coevolutionary standoff between the little and the large. The mitochondrion held on to its ancient DNA, its identity, but even more potently it held the protein that could initiate cell death or apoptosis of the larger cell.

Think of this model of cellular evolution as a metaphor of cultural evolution for entities such as Palestine within Israel, or Ireland within Great Britain and now Europe. Humanity has not yet learned this lesson of life, so the large still seeks to eliminate the little. Eventually humanity will learn or the little will initiate the apoptosis of the large, as Ireland did in the case of the old-fashioned twentieth-century British Empire. But remember that Ireland became part of the European Common Market before the United Kingdom did, so there is a complex architecture to symbiotic coevolution.

When humanity drifted from gathering toward gardening, and then to urban agriculture, a traditional way of life was displaced. The sixth year is the time we track this development, so we can consider this cultural phenomenology of the displaced to be a theme that runs from agriculturalization to technological planetization in terms of the following table.

Cultural Phenomenology of the Displaced

Fifth Grade—The Displaced: Women

If village agriculture is the domestication of plants, city-state agriculture, with its phallic plow and seminal vesicles of the new irrigation system, is the domestication of women. The goddess Inanna comes to the male god of water, Enki (the word for "water" in Sumerian also means "semen"), and complains, "I, the woman, where are my prerogatives?" Enki answers, "Enki perfected greatly that which was woman's work"—meaning, of course, that woman's casual gathering and gardening had now become big-time agribusiness in the hydraulic systems of state irrigation. Inanna tries to answer, but Enki cuts her off by proclaiming, "Lo, the inundation has come." Evidently he held up his penis, and out flowed the Tigris and Euphrates. What's a girl to do?

Sixth Grade—The Displaced: The Shaman

Storage of grain in the temple meant the hybrid crossing of wealth and religious status. The shaman, as prehistoric weatherman, was no longer called upon to prevent starvation. The response of the displaced and powerless was to show that their individual ability to contact divinity had not gone away with the rise in property values of religious real estate. And so we see "the return of the repressed." Moses challenges the high priests of Pharaoh, but he quickly has his charisma routinized by the Aaronitic priesthood—who are in turn challenged by another age of prophets ranting against being "at ease in Zion." As King Solomon becomes a mini-Pharaoh, and Nathan becomes a palace live-in prophet like Henry Kissinger, Elijah, Amos, and Jeremiah get all worked up about this monopoly religion in which you can only pray to God by facing toward King Solomon's temple.

Meanwhile, over in India the yogis in the *Upanishads* are saying "Enough of this Horse Sacrifice nonsense of the Brahmins," and start heading out for the Himalayas and local caves to contact God on their own, without consent of, or consort to, the Brahmin priestly class. Samkhya psychology goes deep into the mind; the Buddha picks up on this and really starts to put the Brahmin priests out of business, so they get even by chasing Buddhism out of India. And over in China, Lao Tzu gets disgusted with all the court politics, becomes an anarchist celebrating the eternal feminine sacrality that stood before the state, and heads out for the wilderness. But Confucius jumps in to the vacancy, becomes a chief of police, and tries to set up a new system of filial piety that will keep Lao Tzu's eternal feminine waiting in the boonies of history until Goethe comes along and picks up on it. Just to make sure that Lao Tzu doesn't mess things up, a bunch of Confucians calling themselves neo-Taoists come in and set up a new business of priestcraft, feng shui, and other necessities that can be traded for a price. Meanwhile, on the other side of the pond, Quetzalcoatl is trying to get rid of the Olmec practice of human sacrifice (probably of fetuses, judging by the statuary) and he is able to expand from La Venta to Teotihuacán. But the black magicians come back with a vengeance, and before you know it the iconography of Quetzalcoatl at Chichén Itzá is decorating, rather than serving to eliminate, human sacrifice.

Seventh Grade—The Displaced: The Prophet

God and his prophet are fine in their place, which may be heaven, the wilderness, or the cave, but it is definitely not the palace, or politics in general. Just as FDR saved capitalism from revolution, and Nehru put Gandhi's picture up on every school wall even as he went on to forget about spinning wheels and developed capital-intensive economies of scale, so did the priests and warriors get together to work out the New Deal of imperialism. But it was a tradeoff. Gone was Assyrian state terrorism of flaying people alive, and arrived was a new and more civilized form of violence in harmony with a new moral order—read that as "moral/order."

Eighth Grade—The Displaced: The Heretic

If morality and force were a delicate balancing act in the new universalizing empires with their moral/order, one could not have some visionary challenging the market share worked out between king and priest in the palace. Brand-name market share for a state religion required eliminating the threat from Gnostics, Manichaeans, Shi'ites, Albigensians, or whoever came along with a personal revelation. So the Pope invented the crusade, learning *jihad* from his Islamic cousins, and aimed it back at them. Seeing how well this worked, St. Bernard of Clairvaux aimed it at the Albigensians. That genocide worked so well that the crusade was reinvented and aimed, not at infidels and heretics, but in defense of the papacy itself. Don't blink now, or you just might miss the birth of the Inquisition.

Ninth Grade—The Displaced: The African Slave

When the New World Indians started dying off from smallpox, nobody was left to mine the gold and silver or cut and refine the cane, so the newly emerging industrial mentality was applied to the old medieval form of slavery to transform it into a capital-intensive economy of scale. Before, in the high baroque of Aphra Behn's *Oroonoco,* your African king was a nobleman who dwelled in a palace and bathed in marble like any Roman Caesar, but the change in scale precipitated a change in quality, and race now was reconstructed as racism—an ideology that would challenge the poor for their position at the bottom of European society.

Tenth Grade—The Displaced: The Poor

Although the African had been seen as a gentleman and prince of nature, the poor in Europe had always been seen as subhuman. So the accumulation of wealth in the new baroque economy of slavery and gaudy display created a new category: class. From the Peasant Wars of the Reformation to the Enclosure Acts in England, the Highland Clearances in Scotland, and the Famine in Ireland, the poor were considered subhuman. The educated were appalled when Wordsworth dared to suggest that "the language of common men in a state of vivid sensation" was an appropriate vehicle for poetry in polite society. When the poor were displaced from the Old World to the New, they fought for a place at the bottom by adopting racism to demonize both redman and black. From Oklahoma Sooners trying to displace the Cherokee to get their lands for family farms to the Draft Riots in Civil War New York, the Scotch-Irish turn on the other "races" in an effort to efface the efficacy of "class" in determining membership in the new republic.

Eleventh Grade—The Displaced: Nature and Culture

From the Industrial Revolution, which introduced industrial pollution and the displacement of traditional cultures, to the rise of genetic engineering and artificial intelligence, which is now about to introduce evolutionary pollution in the form of transgenic organ transplant viral diseases, both nature and culture are being surrounded and compressed in our new baroque economy of hypercapitalism. Due to a consolidation of entertainment, sports, television, politics, and multinational corporate edu-business, the wretched of the Earth got cable, were happy at their work, and voted for the celebrity of their choice who was most successful in fund-raising and able to produce the best commercials.

Notes

Chapter One

1. See Herman Kahn and Anthony Weiner, *The Year 2000* (New York: Macmillan, 1967); also Aubrey Burl, *Avebury* (New Haven, CT: Yale University Press, 1980). Burl continues the intellectual traditions of Glynn Daniel and R. J. C. Atkinson in seeing the makers of Stonehenge and Avebury as superstitious savages whose lives were nasty, brutish, and short. Burl ridicules Alexander Thom's archaeoastronomical studies of the complex geometries of the stone circles as a lot of nonsense, of "Einstein in a sheepskin." The art historians, as opposed to the archaeologists, are much more sensitive, and sensible, in dealing with other worldviews. See, for example, Michael Dames's *Silbury Treasure* (London: Thames and Hudson, 1976) or Keith Critchlow's *Time Stands Still: New Light on Megalithic Science* (London: Gordon Fraser, 1979). One archaeologist within a university department who showed an art historian's sensitivity in reading imagery was UCLA's Marija Gimbutas; see her *Gods and Goddesses of Old Europe* (London: Thames and Hudson, 1974).

2. Werner Heisenberg, "The Representation of Nature in Contemporary Physics," in *Symbolism in Religion and Literature,* ed. Rollo May (New York: Macmillan, 1960), p. 209.

3. From Saussure to Barthes to Lévi-Strauss to Foucault to Derrida, French thinking is textual analysis. Derrida is more open to German and American thinking than most Frenchmen, but his worldview is French, and his famous statement *"Il n'y a dehors texte"* sums up the approach. The old dreary battle between British Empiricism and Continental Rationalism lives on: the Anglo-Americans favoring perception and neorealism, the Continental Europeans favoring perception seen as the *reading* of signs and texts. The French do not take in Asian thought; so Keiji Nishitani's invocation of Dogen's "dropping off of body and mind" would be inconceivable to them. Curiously, however, Francisco Varela has been enthusiastically received in Paris, but the French tend to ignore his interest in Buddhism and read him simply as an exponent of "self-organizing systems biology," for this approach yields maps and recursive diagrams and these can be read as *texts*.

4. Keiji Nishitani, *Religion and Emptiness* (Berkeley, CA: University of California Press, 1982), p. 285.

5. For an interesting approach to the Pacific Shift in philosophy, one that moves from Nagarjuna to Nishitani, Heidegger to Derrida, see Evan Thompson's "Planetary Thinking, Planetary Building: An Essay on Martin Heidegger and Nishitani Keiji," *Philosophy East and West* 36 (3) (1986): 235–252 (Honolulu, HI: University of Hawaii).

6. See Francisco Varela's refutation of representationism in "Living Ways of Sense-Making: A Middle Path for Neuroscience" in *Disorder and Order,* ed.

P. Livingston (Palo Alto, CA: Stanford University Press, 1985). See also Humberto Maturana and Francisco Varela, *El arbol del conocimiento* (Santiago, Chile: Editorial Universitaria, 1984), p. 89.

7. For a history of the Macy Conferences, see Jean-Pierre Dupuy, *The Mechanization of the Mind: On the Origins of Cognitive Science* (Princeton, NJ: Princeton University Press, 2000), pp. 75–89.

8. Gregory Bateson, *Mind and Nature* (New York: E. P. Dutton, 1979), p. 29.

9. Gregory Bateson, *Steps to an Ecology of Mind* (New York: Ballantine, 1972), p. 444.

10. Russell Schweickart, "No Frames, No Boundaries" in *Earth's Answer: Explorations of Planetary Culture at the Lindisfarne Conferences* (New York: Harper & Row, 1977), p. 11.

11. See Bateson, *Steps to an Ecology of Mind*, p. 432.

12. Michel Foucault, *The Order of Things* (New York: Vintage, 1973), p. xxii.

13. See William Irwin Thompson, *Evil and World Order* (New York: Harper & Row, 1977), p. 16.

14. See "Turner traduit Carnot" in Michel Serres, *Hermes III: La Traduction* (Paris: Éditions de Minuit, 1974). The work of Michel Serres interests me for several reasons. First, it is a confirmation of my own approach in taking myth seriously. Second, without knowing of one another's works, we were making similar points in our public lectures in the seventies—*The Time Falling Bodies Take to Light: Mythology, Sexuality, and the Origins of Culture* (New York: St. Martin's Press, 1981) is the text of lectures I gave in New York in the fall of 1976. Third, his literary approach to philosophy is an example of the genre I have elsewhere termed *Wissenskunst* (knowledge as an art form).

15. From a talk by Gary Snyder to the Lindisfarne Fellows Gathering, Zen Center, Green Gulch Farm, Marin County, California, June 1980.

16. Immanuel Wallerstein, *The Modern World-System, vol. I, The Rise of Capitalist Agriculture in the Sixteenth Century* (New York: Academic Press, 1974), p. 348.

17. Michel Serres, *Hermes V: Le Passage du Nord-Ouest* (Paris: Éditions de Minuit, 1980), p. 194. "L'origine de la géometrie est plongée dans l'histoire sacrificielle et les deux parallèles sont désormais en connexion. La légende, le mythe, l'histoire, la philosophie, et la science pure ont des bords communs sur quoi un schéma unitaire construit des ponts."

18. Thompson, *The Time Falling Bodies Take to Light*, p. 96.

19. See Alexander Thom, *Megalithic Lunar Observatories* (Oxford: Oxford University Press, 1971). See also Michael Dames, *The Silbury Treasure* (London: Thames & Hudson, 1976).

20. Kathleen Freeman, *Ancilla to the Pre-Socratics* (Cambridge, MA: Harvard University Press, 1962), p. 19.

21. See Samuel Noah Kramer and Diane Wolkstein, *Inanna: Queen of Heaven* (New York: Harper & Row, 1983).

22. See Thompson, *The Time Falling Bodies Take to Light*, p. 167.

23. Claude Lévi-Strauss, "The Structural Study of Myth," in *Structural Anthropology* (New York: Basic Books, 1963), p. 58.

24. Julian Jaynes, *The Origins of Consciousness in the Breakdown of the Bicameral Mind* (Boston: Houghton Mifflin, 1976).

25. One of the best refutations of the simplistic thinking of the correlation of states of consciousness to discrete physical locations in the brain is to be found in Maturana and Varela's *Autopoiesis and Cognition*, Boston University Studies in the Philosophy of Science, vol. 42 (Bordrect, Holland: Reidl and Co., 1980). Varela has also elaborated his own approach in *Principles of Biological Autonomy* (New York: Elsevier-Holland, 1979).

26. Erich Kahler, *The Tower and the Abyss* (New York: Praeger, 1956).

27. Marshall McLuhan, interview, *Playboy,* March 1969.

28. See David Spangler's *Emergence: The Rebirth of the Sacred* (New York: Dell, 1984). The postreligious spirituality of New Age thinkers such as David Spangler is interpreted by Christian fundamentalists as the Antichrist, and on the Christian cable television channel in the United States, David Spangler and Marilyn Ferguson have been singled out for abusive caricatures of their religious beliefs. The shrillness of Constance Cumbey's paranoid declamations should be compared with the quiet, sane, and unpretentious tone of Spangler's book.

29. The narratives we tell about the creation of the universe and the origin of life tell us about the articulation of order within a specific cultural-ecology. For the Riverine cultural-ecology, as expressed in the Babylonian *Enuma Elish*, the unfoldment of the world is a movement from the prehistoric Great Mother to the historic Great Father, from chaos to polis, from entropy to order in the power of the word. This Babylonian archetypal narrative can be seen to be lurking behind works as different as Genesis or Aeschylus' *Oresteia*. The male consort to the Great Mother is seen to be a particularly horrible abomination to the masculine hero of the new patriarchal order. Kingu is abominable to Marduk in the much the same way that Aegisthus is abominable to Agamemnon and Orestes. This archetypal figure is a historic vestige of the old prehistoric conflict between the mother's brother of matrilineal society and the father and son of patrilineal society.

The *Oresteia* is also similar to the *Enuma Elish* in that it is a narrative of cosmic unfoldment from chaos to polis in which the female is seen to be dark, bloody, and regressive, whereas the male is seen to be light, rational, and progressive. The Babylonian poem ends with a celebration of the city; the Greek play ends with a celebration of the law courts of Athens. The isomorphisms between the two works are fascinating, but since Greek artisans worked on the temples of Persepolis, we should realize that people and ideas traveled more in the Old World than we are in the habit of recognizing.

The basic cosmogonic narrative for the Atlantic cultural-ecology is, of course, Darwin's; but to be fair to precursors, I should point out that Robert Chambers's *Vestiges of Creation* was really the earlier mythic narrative of evolution, and it preceded *On the Origin of Species* by fifteen years, for it was published in London in 1844.

Lest literary intellectuals of the Atlantic epoch in New York rush to attack me for listing Walt Disney's *Fantasia* alongside Hesiod's *Theogony* and Darwin's *Origin,* let me be quick to say that I am not claiming that it is intellectually or artistically equal to them. I am saying that in its vision of evolution wed to

classical music—in the setting for Stravinsky's *Rite of Spring*—it is prophetic of
a visualization of thinking that I believe is going to replace the literate sensibility
of the "Gutenberg Galaxy," and that its mythologizing of the previous scientific
narratives of evolution is characteristic of a new sensibility in which myth and
science are combined. Michel Serres's work, my own *The Time Falling Bodies
Take to Light,* and Philip Glass's scores for *Koyaanisqaatsi* and *Akhenaton*
are all expressions of this sensibility. Whether one wishes to label this new
sensibility "postmodernist" or "New Age" is a matter of affiliation to different
subcultures. Academics and subscribers to *The New York Review of Books*
use the term "postmodernist"; nonacademics and Greens, the subscribers to
Resurgence or *New Age Journal,* seem to prefer the implicit chiliasm of "New
Age." From my point of view, "postmodernist" is a nihilist and deficient form
of the reductionist Galilean Dynamical Mentality, and "New Age" is a cultural
retrieval of the archaic mentalities that had been rendered obsolescent by the
project of modernism.

Chapter Two

    1. Eörs Szathmary and John Maynard Smith, "The Major Evolutionary
Transitions," *Nature,* March 16, 1995, p. 227.

    2. See Brian Greene, *The Elegant Universe: Superstrings, Hidden Di-
mensions, and the Quest for the Ultimate Theory* (New York: Norton,
1999).

    3. For a description of the concept of "natural drift," see Humberto Mat-
urana and Francisco Varela, *The Tree of Knowledge: The Biological Roots of
Human Understanding* (Boston: New Science, 1987), pp. 93–121.

    4. Consider Darwin's own narrative from the conclusion to *On the Origin
of Species:* "And as natural selection works solely by and for the good of each
being, all corporeal and mental endowments will tend to progress towards
perfection"; quoted in *Darwin: A Norton Critical Edition,* ed. Philip Appleman
(New York: Norton, 1970), p. 198. For a discussion of nineteenth-century
narratives of connection and causation, see also Gillian Beer, *Darwin's Plots*
(London: Routledge, 1984).

    5. Jane Jacobs, *The Economy of Cities* (New York: Vintage, 1970).

    6. A wonderful study of this form of cultural evolution is Jered Diamond's
Guns, Germs, and Steel: The Fate of Human Societies (New York: Norton,
1997).

    7. This approach to cultural history has been developed in collaboration
with a new group of biologists and philosophers of science. Teachers unfamil-
iar with this approach should consult the books of Francisco Varela, James
Lovelock, Lynn Margulis, Susan Oyama, Evan Thompson, and Stuart Kauffman. A book of conference papers in which many of these scientists can be
found is *Gaia Two: Emergence, The New Science of Becoming,* ed. William
Irwin Thompson (Hudson, NY: Lindisfarne, 1991).

    8. A shift from linear systems of cause and effect appeared in many places
simultaneously, from General Systems Theory in Europe to the Macy Conferences in New York, but certainly the early work of Gregory Bateson in the
thirties, later published as *Naven* (Palo Alto, CA: Stanford University Press,

1956), was one of these articulations of the study of the feedback of the effect on the cause that creates a new and more complex causal set. I used Bateson's work in my undergraduate honors thesis in 1962. Later when I established the Lindisfarne Association, I invited Bateson to become our scholar in residence in 1976 and 1977 while he was at work on *Mind in Nature*. In 1977, Bateson and I organized a Lindisfarne conference on this theme for which we invited the young Chilean biologist Francisco Varela to take part. He became Lindisfarne's next scholar in residence as he worked on the publication of his early articulation of complex dynamical systems in his book, *Principles of Biological Autonomy*. After Bateson's death, I organized a Lindisfarne conference in 1981 in which we brought together the Santiago school of biology with Humberto Maturana and Varela, and the exponents of the then-new Gaian theory, James Lovelock and Lynn Margulis, as well as the exponent of the French school of self-organizing systems, Henri Atlan. This conference was subsequently published as *Gaia: A Way of Knowing* (Hudson, NY: Lindisfarne, 1987). In 1988, at the invitation of the government of the Province of Perugia and Umbria, I organized a followup conference on emergence and self-organizing systems with this group, and others, and this became the second volume, *Gaia Two*. For the twentieth anniversary of Lindisfarne, we invited Stuart Kauffman from the Santa Fe Institute to participate in discussions with Francisco Varela and the other Lindisfarne Fellows. Kauffman joined the Fellowship at that time and now serves on Lindisfarne's board of directors. One can see that from the early work of Bateson and the Macy Conferences to Lindisfarne and the Santa Fe Institute is a direct line of development in which the philosophers are carrying on the philosophical discussions in a face-to-face manner in the cultural dynamic of the small conference that Bateson in particular so dearly loved.

9. See Jean Gebser, *The Ever-Present Origin*, trans. Noel Barstad and Algis Mickunas (Athens, OH: Ohio University Press, 1991).

10. An earlier version of the preceding pages appears in my essay, "Our Contemporary Predicament and the Present Evolution of Consciousness" in *Coming into Being: Artifacts and Texts in the Evolution of Consciousness* (New York: St. Martin's Press, 1996).

Chapter Three

1. See Ray Kurzweil, *The Age of Spiritual Machines* (New York: Viking, 1999); also Hans Moravec, *Mind Children: The Future of Robot and Human Intelligence* (Cambridge, MA: Harvard University Press, 1988).

2. I argue this point at greater length in "The Past Evolution of Consciousness: From Spirochete to Spinal Cord," in *Coming into Being: Artifacts and Texts in the Evolution of Consciousness* (New York: St. Martin's Press, 1996), pp. 17–44.

3. See E. R. Dodds's "From Shame-Culture to Guilt-Culture" in *The Greeks and the Irrational* (Berkeley, CA: University of California Press, 1951), pp. 28–63.

4. Leon Botstein, "Let Teen-Agers Try Adulthood," op-ed essay, *The New York Times*, May 17, 1999, p. A21.

5. William Irwin Thompson, *Passages about Earth: An Exploration of the New Planetary Culture* (New York: Harper & Row, 1974), p. 21.

Chapter Four

1. Gebser, p. 41.

2. William Irwin Thompson, *Imaginary Landscape: Making Worlds of Myth and Science* (New York: St. Martin's Press, 1989), pp. 3–42.

3. Remo H. Largo, *Die Kinderjahre* (Zurich: Piper Verlag, 1999). There is also evidence that in mammals the close bonding, nursing, and fondling of mother and infant serves to activate gene expression and select for a healthy organism with a fully functional immune system. See M. J. Meany et al., "Early Environmental Regulation of Forebrain Glucocorticoid Receptor Gene Expression: Implications for Adrenocortical Responses to Stress," *Developmental Neuroscience* 18 (1996), pp. 49–72.

4. Leonard Shlain, *The Alphabet versus the Goddess: The Conflict between Word and Image* (New York: Viking, 1998).

5. For a discussion of the negative side effects and permanent neurological damage done to children through the overprescription of psychostimulant drugs, see Jaak Panksepp, *Affective Neuroscience: The Foundations of Human and Animal Emotions* (New York: Oxford University Press, 1998), pp. 320–323.

6. Robert Graves, *The White Goddess* (New York: Farrar, Straus, & Giroux, 1975), chapters 10 and 11, "The Tree Alphabet (1) and (2)."

7. Lawrence Kushner, *The Book of Letters: A Mystical Alef-Bait* (New York: Jewish Lights, 1991).

8. Stan Tenen, *A Matrix of Meaning for Sacred Alphabets,* videotape (San Anselmo, CA: Meru Foundation, 1991).

9. For a comparison of the evolution of the early city in China and Mesoamerica, see Paul Wheatley, *The Pivot of the Four Quarters* (Chicago: Aldine, 1971).

10. A. F. Aveni, *World Archaeoastronomy* (London: Cambridge University Press, 1989).

11. *The Exaltation of Inanna,* eds. William W. Hallo and J. A. Van Dijk (New Haven, CT: Yale University Press, 1968).

12. Shlain.

13. For a discussion of these two works, see my book *The Time Falling Bodies Take to Light.*

14. See George G. Joseph, *The Crest of the Peacock: The Non-European Roots of Mathematics* (London: Tauris, 1991).

15. Sappho Fragment 185; in Willis Barnstone, *Sappho and the Greek Lyric Poets* (New York: Schocken, 1962), p. 80.

16. See Merlin Stone's *When God Was a Woman* (New York: Dial Press, 1976).

17. See Derek A. Welsby, *The Kingdom of Kush: The Natapan and Meroitic Empires* (Princeton, NJ: Markus Wiener, 1998).

18. For a less mystical approach to the Axial Age, see Gore Vidal's novel *Creation* (New York: Ballantine, 1981).

19. See *The Upanishads,* trans. Eknath Easwaran (Tomales, CA: Nilgiri Press, 1987), p. 111.

20. *The Dhammapada: The Sayings of Buddha,* translation and commentary by Thomas Cleary (New York: Bantam Books, 1995).

21. Lao Tzu, *Te-Tao Ching,* trans. R. G. Henricks (New York: Ballantine Books, 1989). For a discussion of Lao Tzu's work as a revival of the prehistoric goddess religion, see the chapter "The Road Not Taken" in my *Coming into Being: Artifacts and Texts in the Evolution of Consciousness* (New York: St. Martin's Press, 1998).

22. *The Essential Confucius,* trans. Thomas Cleary (San Francisco: Harper-SanFrancisco, 1992).

23. For translations and introductory essay, see my *Blue Jade from the Morning Star: A Cycle of Poems and an Essay on Quetzalcoatl* (Hudson, NY: Lindisfarne, 1983). For a different interpretation, see Enrique Florescano's *Myth of Quetzalcoatl* (Baltimore, MD: Johns Hopkins University Press, 1999); see page 135 for his discussion of Olmec ceremonial centers. For the presence of the iconography of the Plumed Serpent in Olmec culture, see *The Olmec World: Ritual and Rulership,* ed. Jill Guthrie (Princeton, NJ: Princeton University Art Museum, 1996), p. 84. My own highly poetic and speculative interpretation is that the poetry and the artifacts show a conflict between an archaic shamanic tradition and an emergent prophetic religion. In the archaic tradition of animal possession, the shaman projects his subtle body into a jaguar and brings about the birth of a half-human, half-jaguar baby. To propitiate this spirit, human sacrifice of fetuses in the womb are offered up—hence the presence of all these infants with jaguar features. Quetzalcoatl tries to suppress this tradition with a higher morality, and he establishes his palace and temple, but the sorcerers come to bring him down and return to their archaic ways of human sacrifice.

24. See Cyrus Gordon, *Before Columbus* (New York: Crown, 1971), and Barry Fell, *America B.C.* (New York: Quadrangle, 1977), also Ivan Van Sertima, *They Came Before Columbus: The African Presence in Ancient America* (New York: Random House, 1977).

25. Consult the works of Harold Innis, Marshall McLuhan, Eric Havelock, and Leonard Shlain for discussions of the role of the alphabet in the formation of Greek society.

26. For an alternative to the party line on Plato, see Adriana Cavarero's *In Spite of Plato: A Feminist Rewriting of Ancient Philosophy* (New York: Routledge, 1995).

27. See Richard C. Foltz, *Religions of the Silk Road* (New York: St. Martin's Press, 1999).

28. See Amin Malouf, *The Crusades through Arab Eyes* (New York: Schocken Books, 1989). An excellent globalist view of the interacting world civilizations of this time can be found in Archibald Lewis's *Nomads and Crusaders, AD 1000–1368* (Bloomington, IN: Indiana University Press, 1988).

29. The helmet of the knight in the paintings of this book bears the emblematic device of a winged heart, which is the primary icon of Sufism. See *King René's Book of Love* (New York: Braziller, 1980).

30. Alfred W. Crosby sees this shift as occurring before the Renaissance. "Then, between 1250 and 1350, there came, not so much in theory as in actual

application, a marked shift. We can probably pare that century down to fifty years, 1275 to 1325." See his *Measure of Reality: Quantification and Western Society, 1250–1600* (Cambridge, UK: Cambridge University Press, 1997), p. 18. Since this is the time of Giotto and Dante, it makes some sense to see the intellectual breakthrough occurring then, followed by the calamity of the Black Death, and then the economic and social reconstruction of Europe that we associate with Florentine capitalism and Renaissance art. Cultural historians as different as Alfred Crosby and Rudolf Steiner both see the thirteenth century as the time of the bifurcation in the evolution of consciousness, so perhaps it is more informed to push the Renaissance back, before the Black Death. The new mentality would then be seen to be expressed in Arabic music and poetry, inspiring Provençal poetry and Dante's *dolce stil nuovo,* as well as the new mathematical sensibility. The Algebraic Mentality could then be seen as a transition state between the Geometrical and the Galilean Dynamical to come. Unlike the Geometrical Mentality, however, the Algebraic is too esoteric and does not externalize itself as an entire civilization with its corresponding architectural monuments.

31. William H. McNeill, *Plagues and Peoples* (Chicago: University of Chicago Press, 1984).

32. See Gottfried Wilhelm Leibniz, *Discourse on the Natural Theology of the Chinese* (Honolulu, HI: Monographs of the Society for Asian and Comparative Philosophy, No. 4, University of Hawaii Press, 1977).

33. My sense of cultural history has been influenced by Ferdnand Braudel (surely the twentieth century's greatest cultural historian) and Immanuel Wallerstein. For example, Braudel states: "When in 1421 the Ming rulers of China changed their capital city—leaving Nanking, and moving to Peking, in order to face the dangers of the Manchu and Mongol frontier—the massive world-economy of China swung round for good, turning its back on a form of economic activity based on ease of access to seaborne trade. A new landlocked metropolis was now established deep in the interior and began to draw everything towards it. Whether conscious or unconscious, this choice was decisive. In the race for world dominion, this was the moment when China lost her position in a contest she had entered without fully realizing it, when she had launched the first maritime expeditions from Nanking in the early fifteenth century." See Ferdnand Braudel, *Civilization and Capitalism, Volume III: The Perspective of the World* (London: Fontana, 1984), p. 32.

34. See Robin Blackburn, *The Making of New World Slavery* (London: Verso, 1997).

35. Patricia Buckley Ebrey, *Cambridge Illustrated History of China* (London: Cambridge University Press, 1996), p. 209.

36. Lisa Jardine, *Worldly Goods: A New History of the Renaissance* (London: Macmillan, 1996), pp. 370–376.

37. A good work to consult here is Frances Yates's *The Rosicrucian Enlightenment* (London: Routledge, 1972).

38. Ibid.

39. See *The Beethoven Quartet Companion,* ed. Robert Winter and Robert Martin (Los Angeles: University of California Press, 1994), pp. 11–27.

40. See Jacques Attali, *Noise: The Political Economy of Music* (Minneapolis, MN: University of Minnesota Press, 1985), pp. 31, 32.

41. See Michel Serres, "Turner traduit Carnot."

42. See Ferdnand Braudel, *Civilization and Capitalism: The Perspective of the World*, p. 272.

43. See "War, Money, and the Nation-State," in Paul Kennedy's *Rise and Fall of the Great Powers: 1500 to 2000* (New York: Random House, 1988). See also Braudel's "England's Greatness and the National Debt," in *Civilization and Capitalism: The Perspective of the World*, pp. 375–379; and Simon Schama, *The Embarrassment of Riches: An Interpretation of Dutch Culture in the Golden Age* (New York: Knopf, 1987).

44. Thomas Babington Macaulay, *The History of England* (London: Penguin, 1979), pp. 488, 505.

45. See E. P. Thompson's classic, *The Making of the English Working Class* (New York: Random House, 1966).

46. Paul Kennedy, p. 109.

47. For an understanding of Blake's dissenting background, with its antinomian rejection of polite bourgeois culture, see E. P. Thompson, *Witness against the Beast: William Blake and the Moral Law* (New York: New Press, 1993).

48. See John A. Crow, *The Epic of Latin America* (Berkeley, CA: University of California Press, 1992), p. 436.

49. I think the best (and briefest) study of this social phenomenon is still A. F. C. Wallace's classic paper from almost a half-century ago, "Revitalization Movements," *American Anthropologist* 85 (April 1956), pp. 264–281. This paper used to be available in the journal's reprint series.

50. See Eleanor Rosch, Evan Thompson, and Francisco Varela, *The Embodied Mind: Cognitive Science and Human Experience* (Cambridge, MA: MIT Press, 1991); also Thompson and Varela's *Why the Mind Is Not in the Head* (Cambridge, MA: Harvard University Press, in press).

51. David Jordan, *Transforming Paris: The Life and Labors of Baron Haussmann* (Chicago: University of Chicago Press, 1995), p. 172.

52. See Juliet Wilson-Bareau, *Manet, Monet, and the Gare Saint-Lazare* (New Haven, CT: Yale University Press, 1998).

53. See Giulio M. Gallarotti, *The Anatomy of an International Monetary Regime: The Classical Gold Standard, 1880–1914* (New York: Oxford University Press, 1995).

54. See Thomas Pakenham, *The Scramble for Africa: The White Man's Conquest of the Dark Continent from 1876 to 1912* (New York: Avon Books, 1993), p. 311.

55. See Lewis P. Curtis Jr., *Apes and Angels: The Irishman in Victorian Caricature* (New York: Braziller, 1971); also Noel Ignatiev, *How the Irish Became White* (New York: Routledge, 1995).

56. For a fascinating study of the relationships between science and art in the twentieth century, one written by a world-famous scientist, see C. H. Waddington's *Behind Appearance: A Study of the Relations between Painting and the Natural Sciences in This Century* (Edinburgh: University of Edinburgh

Press, 1969). See also Arthur I. Miller's *Einstein, Picasso: Space, Time, and the Beauty That Causes Havoc* (New York: Basic Books, 2001).

57. See Michael J. Hogan, *A Cross of Iron: Harry S. Truman and the Origins of the National Security State, 1945–1954* (New York: Cambridge University Press, 1998).

58. See Samuel Noah Kramer, *The Sumerians: Their History, Culture, and Character* (Chicago: University of Chicago Press, 1963), p. 116.

59. Walter Benjamin, "Paris, die Hauptstadt des XIX Jahrhunderts," *Illuminationen: Ausgewählte Schriften* (Frankfurt am Main: Suhrkamp, 1974), 170–184.

60. See Gallarotti.

61. See *Frantisek Kupka: Die Abstrakten Farben des Universums,* ed. Dorothy Kosinski and Jaroslav Andel (Ostfildern bei Stuttgart, Germany: Verlag Gerd Hatje, 1998).

62. On more than one occasion, younger scholars have accused me of using the ideas of Baudrillard without due citation. My approach to writing on contemporary culture was certainly influenced by Marshall McLuhan, whom I encountered both at MIT and the University of Toronto, but my writings on Los Angeles came twenty years before I read Baudrillard. In 1967, I wrote "Los Angeles: Reflections at the Edge of History," which was published in *The Antioch Review* in 1968; it became the first chapter of my book *At the Edge of History* in 1971. Because this book was nominated for the National Book Award, it was translated into popular editions in French and Italian, where both Baudrillard and Eco could easily encounter it. I went on to write on Disneyland and fake history in the introduction to the 1988 reissue of this book and in my subsequent work, *The American Replacement of Nature* (New York: Doubleday, 1991). I now delight in Baudrillard's outrageously French and his own arrogantly footnoteless style, but my approach comes from having grown up in Los Angeles and having been a teenager with a car at the time of the opening of Disneyland.

63. Braudel's perception of this shift is brilliant. "Can one suggest that a highly convenient rule might operate in this context, to wit, that any city which is becoming or has become the centre of a world-economy, is the first place in which the seismic movements of the system show themselves, and subsequently the first to be truly cured of them? If so, it would shed a new light on Black Thursday in Wall Street in 1929, which I am inclined to see as marking the *beginning* of New York's leadership of the world"; Braudel, p. 272.

64. Pierre Teilhard de Chardin, *The Future of Man* (New York: Harper & Row, 1964), p. 130.

65. See Nancy Jack Todd and John Todd, *From Eco-Cities to Living Machines: Principles of Ecological Design* (Berkeley, CA: North Atlantic Books, 1994).

Index